The Diary of an Irish Countryman
1827–1835

The Diary
of an
Irish Countryman
1827–1835

A Translation of
Cín Lae Amhlaoibh

by
Tomás de Bhaldraithe

MERCIER PRESS

Mercier Press
PO Box 5, 5 French Church Street, Cork
24 Lower Abbey Street, Dublin 1

© Tomás de Bhaldraithe, 1979

Cín Lae Amhlaoibh edited by Tomás de Bhaldraithe was first
published in 1970 by An Clóchomhar Teoranta.

This book was originally published in 1979 by Mercier Press
under the title *The Diary Of Humphrey O'Sullivan*.

ISBN: 1 85635 042 8

Printed in Ireland by Colour Books Ltd.

CONTENTS

PREFACE

This book is a translation of *Cín Lae Amhlaoibh* (Dublin 1970), a selection from Amhlaoibh Ó Súilleabháin's diary which covered the period 1827-35.

The translator (who is also the editor of *Cín Lae Amhlaoibh*) while trying to remain faithful to the original, avoided a slavish word for word translation. He was well aware that the style of good writing in one language cannot be adequately reproduced in another and in particular that any attempt to render in English the pithiness, rime or rhythm of Irish proverbs or verses is bound to failure.

It was not easy to decide on a consistent method of dealing with personal and place names. The diarist himself is sometimes inconsistent, on occasion alternating Irish forms with English translations, and vice-versa. As a general rule, place names well-known to the outsider are given here in their Anglicized form, while lesser-known names are left in the original Irish. A compromise has been reached in some cases where it was thought necessary to indicate the nature of the place by adding a generic English term (e.g. Abha Bheag river), although this is obviously tautological to the Irish speaker (as is the 'Isle of Inisfree' where *Inis* means 'isle').

As regards personal names, English forms have been given where the diarist is consistent, and in some other cases where the person was probably better known by the English form.

My thanks are due to the Royal Irish Academy for permission to publish this translation, to David Thomson for reading it and making some valuable suggestions, and to Honóra Ní Chríogáin and Marion Gunn for careful preparation of the typescript.

INTRODUCTION

Amhlaoibh Ó Súilleabháin, the writer of this diary, was born in Killarney, Co. Kerry, in May 1780. Nine years later his father Donncha, a hedge school master, moved with his family to Waterford in search of a better living, and later to Co. Kilkenny, where he settled down near Callan.

Father and son taught school for many years at the Crossroads, in a small cabin which took the neighbours three days to build, as he describes in the diary (14/5/'27).

Amhlaoibh moved in to Callan some years later, perhaps after the death of his father in 1808. He set up a school, which at one period had one hundred and twenty pupils.

By 1824 he seems to have given up teaching, as his school is not mentioned in the comprehensive survey of schools made in that year.[1] His brother's school in Little Bridge Street (which had one hundred and four pupils and an income of fifty pounds a year from them) is mentioned in that report. Perhaps Amhlaoibh taught there.

On the other hand, he is listed in Pigot's *City of Dublin and Hibernian Provincial Directory* (London, 1824), as a 'linen draper'.

He did open his school again some time later, as he refers to it in the diary during May 1829, from which date he notes the arrival and departure of pupils. The number of pupils rose to thirty, and then seems to have fallen, until 1831, when he finally closed the school. It would appear from the diary that his business was prospering and that he was also giving more time to the affairs of the town — *Callainn an Chlampair*, 'Callan of the Ructions', which was noted for its extreme poverty in a country where the great majority of the people lived under wretched conditions.

The English writer Thomas Cromwell refers to Callan as 'the very impersonation of Irish poverty and

1. *First Report of the Commissioners on Irish Education*, London, 1825.

wretchedness' in his *Excursions thro' Ireland III* (London, 1820), and another visitor, H. D. Inglis in *Ireland in 1834* (London, 1835) wrote as follows:

I had not yet seen in Ireland any town in so wretched a condition as this. I arrived in it very early in the morning; and having been promised breakfast at a grocer's shop (for there is no inn in Callan), I walked through the outskirts of the town, and round a little common which lies close to it, and there I saw the people crawling out of their hovels — they and their hovels not one shade better than I have seen in the sierras of Granada, where the people live in holes excavated in the banks. Their cabins were mere holes, with nothing within them (I speak of two which I entered) excepting a little straw, and one or two broken stools. And all the other outskirts of the town, are in nearly a similar condition — ranges of hovels, without a ray of comfort or a trace of civilisation about them: and people either in a state of actual starvation, or barely keeping body and soul together. All this I saw, and cannot be deceived; and from the inquiries which I made of intelligent persons, the Protestant clergyman among the number, I may state, that in this town, containing between four and five thousand inhabitants, at least one thousand are without regular employment; six or seven hundred entirely destitute; and that there are upwards of two hundred actual medicants in the town — persons incapable of work.

Amhlaoibh was deeply moved by the sufferings of the poor, and was always active in seeking to improve their condition. He was, for example, secretary to a group which opposed Lord Cliften's attempt to clear the cabin-dwellers from the commonage. He took part in the distribution of yellow meal; went bail for a poor *spalpeen* in trouble; collected money to give a decent burial to a beggar woman, and in general showed his sympathy with the oppressed in a practical way.

On the other hand, he often condemns the 'ugly rabble' of the town for fighting, drunkeness, and practising cruel sports such as bull-baiting.

As his business prospered he became an important person in the neighbourhood, and was on friendly terms with the doctor and parish priest, as well as with the members of the Protestant middle class. This helped him in getting signatures to 'The Protestant Declaration in favour of Catholic Emancipation'. He collected the Catholic Rent, addressed public meetings, including the 'monster' meeting at Ballyhale, at which he spoke in Irish.

In an early entry he referred to himself as a *seanchaí*, by which he meant a person well versed in Irish historical lore and literature. That this was no idle claim is borne out by his large collection of Irish manuscripts, many of which were copies made by himself, others which he had annotated.

Soon after his death in 1838, these manuscripts were purchased by Hodges and Smith, the Dublin booksellers, and most of them later found their way to the Royal Irish Academy, where they are now kept. Among them was the manuscript of the diary which he wrote, or rather scribbled in his own erratic spelling, in used school headline copy books, and old account books.

Amhlaoibh the *seanchaí* scarcely appears in the diary, the main inspiration for which seems to have been his interest in nature in general and his delight in the changing scenery of the countryside. In this he was following his own bent, but was also influenced by the current movement as exemplified by the English naturalist Gilbert White of Selborne, who began publishing his notes on natural phenomena towards the end of the century, and whose books had become extremely popular by the first half of the 19th century.[2]

2. A detailed study of the influence on Amhlaoibh of the romantic movement in literature, painting and natural history has been made by Professor Breandán Ó Madagáin in *An Dialann Dúlra* (Dublin 1978).

The keeping of a personal diary was unknown among writers of Irish before Amhlaoibh's time. Prose writing in Irish had almost come to an end with the turn of the century, and publication in Irish was non-existent, except for catechetical matter and some editing of annals or historical tales. Contemporary Irish scholars saw no future for the language and consequently wrote in English.

Amhlaoibh, then, showed remarkable originality and courage in undertaking a diary in the Irish language. He was of course well aware that the language was in danger, but he also realised that it was a vigorous medium of expression with a long unbroken literary tradition, and was still the spoken language of about three million people in Ireland, which number included a fair proportion of the people of County Kilkenny, as evidenced, for example, by William Tighe who wrote:

> English being taught at all schools, it is understood by most of the younger part of the lower classes; but there are many persons, and particularly women, in the hilly districts who cannot speak a word of English: in the hills of Idagh, Irish is said to be tolerable well spoken. The common people seldom speak any other language among themselves; but Irish is more prevalent about Kilkenny and near Munster, than near the county of Carlow. The priests often preach alternately in Irish and English; but always in Irish if they are desirous to be well understood.*(Statistical Observations relative to the County of Kilkenny* (1802)).

Apart then from the diary's value as a human and social document, it was a valuable contribution to Irish writing at a period when prose writing hardly existed. His broad reading of Irish literature in manuscript obviously influenced his style, but he rejected the time-honoured alliterative, turgid, bombastic style of the romantic tales and developed a simple individual style based on current idiom. This was probably not a conscious decision, but rather the result of a busy man jotting down notes as clearly and concisely as possible.

A translation cannot reproduce the style of the original, but it is hoped that this selection will give some insight into the character of a remarkable man, an acute observer, and a person of broad interests, who took an active part in the life of the community.

There are many accounts in English of life in Ireland in the first half of the last century, but most of them are by outsiders who often came with preconceived ideas, or wrote for foreign readers.

The value of Amhlaoibh's work as a social document is that it gives the view of a member of the community, who found himself in the unusual position of being on familiar terms with people of different classes and of different religions and political allegiance. He also had the great advantage of being bilingual.

The diary is all the more valuable because the writer did not set out to put forward any point of view, nor to attempt a considered description of his neighbours and their way of life. By jotting down notes on daily activities he has left us a lively and frank account of life in a small town during a particularly agitated and important period in Irish history, which included the struggle for Catholic Emancipation, the Tithe War, the foundation of the National Schools, the secret societies, famine, plague, evictions and faction fighting.

In spite of all that, Amhlaoibh managed to live a full life as a successful business man, a fearless worker in the cause of freedom and social justice, a lover of nature, an antiquarian, collector of manuscripts, and enjoyer of good food and drink. He also found time to copy manuscripts, write some tales and sketches, compose some indifferent verses, compile a botanical vocabularly, and to leave us a remarkable contribution to the social history of the country, as seen from the inside by a man of wide interests and deep understanding.

January 1827 . . . *Dark dour gloomy January*. That old saying doesn't suit the month this year. Fine frosty weather we've had this month. Farmers are spreading manure from the headlands. No flowers to be seen except the daisy and the furze blossom, both of which can be seen all throughout the year, however severe the weather.

On the twenty-sixth of the month, I myself, A. Ó Súilleabháin, historian, and Pádraig Céitinn, medical doctor from Callan, walked along the King's River, passed through Caisleán Aoife, a mile and a half from Callan, where I drew a sketch of the castle and its enclosure. We went from there to Ceanannas where I made a sketch of the monastery. I am writing 'The Adventures of —'.[3]

At Muileann an Úcaire, between Muileann Uí Bhriain and Cill Bhriocáin Mills I saw an otter catching fish.

April 1st . . . *Showery April of the fresh bleating*.

I went with the funeral of Seán Ó Riain's aunt to Teampaill Loisc or Cill Train. We left Callan at one o'clock, went through Sceach an Chloithreán, across Cnoc Riabhach and Tulach Mhaoine, through Baile Mhac Dháith to Teampall Loisc, about four Irish miles from Callan.

There is a stone in the graveyard with the date 1552 on it.

The countryside around Teampall Loisc is beautiful. There are pine forests at Teampall Loisc and at Cill Chobhráin. It is a fine country for wheat, oats, barley (two-rowed and four-rowed) and potatoes, although they failed last year because of the drought.

The yellowish blue famine is all over the countryside. Fivepence halfpenny for a miserable stone of potatoes (fourteen pounds to the stone); eighteen shillings for a

3. He evidently had not yet decided the title of the tale.

barrel of oats (fourteen stone to the barrel), and poor people without work or pay to buy any kind of food. There are not even alms for the paupers. They are being sent off home, to their own parishes. Callan's own paupers, who number three hundred families, or fifteen hundred persons, are reduced to misery.

A collection is being made for them by Lord Cliften, the priest and the minister of the parish, the Chief Magistrate and the Callan merchants. But it won't last even half of them for long, God help them.

I took my time coming home. It was a fine soft fresh day.

'We went from there to Ceanannas where I made a sketch of the Monastery'. (p. 15)

2nd ... I set out from Callan at ten o'clock in the morning with Maraed de Barra, a widow, and her sweet-voiced daughter, Maraeidín. Mícheál Ó Cuidithe, a dark bushy-haired fellow, was our driver. He had an old purblind, emaciated, heavy-hoofed, shambling cart-horse.

We passed over Droichead na nGabhar, and went on down by the river to Muileann Uí Bhriain, Baile Mailearta, and Teampall Geal, crossed the Camaisc, continued on to Cathair Leisc, and then to Barr Scuab, where we turned southwards.

The countryside between Callan and Barr Scuab is very beautiful. Wheat is beginning to come on well now. Both sides of the road are well furnished with forests and groves, particularly at Bealach an Tóibín or Bealach an Chabhais. But from Barr Scuab to Ros an Eara the land on either side has a bare look, with pools and the yellow clay to be seen. Sliabh na mBan to the southwest is a beautiful sight under a cap of fog, and the hillocks covered with pine-groves from top to bottom form a chain from Sliabh na mBan to Baile Roibin.

Cill Mogeanna is a pretty country village. A great number of new houses are being built there. The rent of a site and a small garden is only a crown a year. There is good red and yellow stone to be had from the hill at the end of the village, and plenty of slate nearby at Áth na Slinnteacha. We came home quietly and in no hurry, having drunk a small drop of whiskey at Power's inn. The whole day, and particularly the evening, was very pleasant. At the weir at Muileann an Bhrianaigh there is a waterfall and a fine pool, with a willow-grove south of it, and an island with pine trees to the north. The beautiful young girl stood between me and the waterfall, and sang for us, while the waterfall was murmuring and the trees were whispering. She stood like a fairy woman in the spray of the waterfall. My heart was light. Scarlet clouds lay on Sliabh na mBan. They turned from scarlet to yellow, from yellow to greenish, to blue, to black, to jet black. The young girl stopped singing.

7th ... A large market of potatoes, oats, turf and coal. Sixpence a stone for potatoes, from seventeen shillings to a pound a barrel for oats; thirty shillings for wheat at Muileann an Bhrianaigh; ten pence for a hundredweight

of coal, two shillings a small basket of turf from Poll na
Caillí, a halfcrown for the same from Poll an Chapaill;
from fourpence halfpenny to sixpence halfpenny a
hundred for cabbage; fivepence a pot or a pound a
hundredweight for meal . . .

8th . . . A quiet pleasant sunny morning. Just a few thin
clouds to be seen stirring. Fog on the hills and mountains
. . .

A beautiful evening. Went for a walk down the
Mionnán Road, through the Damhasc meadow, through
Gabháltas an Mhionnáin, to the lime-kiln and from there
to the Weir at the west end of Garrán Giúise Island . . .

On my way home across Droichead na nGabhar I
heard on every side the thrush, the lark, and every other
little bird singing to each other. The youths and girls of
the town were out walking through the meadows along by
the King's River.

Went to vespers at the Brothers' Chapel where I heard
heavenly music.

12th . . . I hope to God the people's hearts will soften.
Three hundred families in Callan are starving.

This is the twelfth day of April, the first day of the Old
Brindled Cow's Three Days — three days which the
weather of Old March took from the beginning of Old
April. This is how the old story goes:

There was once upon a time an old brindled cow which
lived through the whole month of March without falling
into a bog-hole and being swallowed up. When the first
day of Old April came, she cocked her tail straight up and
started to run about mooing, so delighted was she that the
fine weather had come and that she had come safe and
sound through all the hardships of 'raw windy cruel
March.' 'Wait, wait,' said Old March's rough weather
and went to talk to the mild weather of 'fresh bleating
showery April,' and asked her for three days.

'I'll give you those,' said April's weather, 'if you marry me.'

'I will indeed,' said the rough old lively fellow to the mild fairy-like April weather. And the cruel fierce wind began to blow from the east over from Scotland and the old brindled cow went to search for some green grass on the top of a swamp and there she was drowned.

That is the story which gave the 'three days of the old brindled cow' their name.

13th ... A gentle south-west wind. Sultry, cloud periods and bright patches. Soft clouds like fleeces on top of each other. From Cill Bhriocáin Mills I saw the Galtees west of Cathair. The eastern mountain looked flat, and the western peak was like the top of a volcano. A thin mist-like foam between me and them. The Déise mountains beckoning to me with their peaks up over Bearna na Gaoithe gap.

A rich land and a poor people. I ask you a question. Why is this?

14th ... The paupers have light hearts as they expect a bite of meat to-morrow. The country people are gathering in for the market. The country cabin-dwellers eat meat on only three days a year, Christmas Day, Shrove Tuesday, and Easter Sunday.

15th Easter Sunday ... A beautiful day. At mid-day five of us left Callan to go to Desart Court. We went through Gráig Amhlaoibh, passed Dair Mhór, prancing through the lord's wood, and Doirín and Úrachillín, until we arrived at the fish ponds at Desart Court. There is a very beautiful view of the countryside from this pleasant mansion. A heat haze. The mountains to the south were dark blue. All around us were thick forests with leafless ash and oak growing among the evergreen pine. The meadows as smooth as silk or satin and as green as corn in the blade. It is an earthly paradise. We headed off to the level ground beside Baile Uí Gheibhle and stopped at

Butler's where we got white loaves, rich bacon, sweet mutton, white pudding, and a drop of the barley juice to drink from the pretty hostess. We went off home in good spirits through Tulach Mhaoine, Cnoc Riabhach, etc. As fine an evening as I ever saw.

16th Easter Monday or Easter-Eggs Day [*Lá na Cúbóige*] . . . A bright sunny calm morning. At mid-day the young girls and young men eating their eggs and drinking in the hostelries. Evening, and the hostelries still full of young people. A very fine day.

17th . . . *Long as the drinking lasts, it ends in thirst. It's sweet drinking, it's bitter paying.* The street mob were very noisy at three in the morning. Some of them are still very drunk. It's no harm to call them 'mob' *(coip)* for they are the froth *(coipeadh)* of the lake-dwellers, bog-dwellers, and dirty mountain-dwellers with no respect or manners . . .

18th . . . At mid-day gay sweet-voiced Maraed de Barra, myself and another person went to Desart Court along the same way I went on Easter Sunday. We walked through the dark evergreen pine woods where we were sheltered from the sun as we went along the fine winding paths which straightened out now and again. We could hear the lark's song in the nearby meadows, the shorter call of the blackbird, the thrush and all the smaller birds which seemed to be in harmony with Maraed de Barra's gentle lively melodious speech. We went astray in a dark shadowy little glen until we couldn't make out east from west or north from south. At long last, having gone through mossy hollows, clumps of brambles, slopes covered with ash trees, and evergreen pine groves, we reached Cluain Lachan with its ponds, pools, lakelets, streams and murmuring waterfalls. White ducks and spotted drakes were there, and the blackbirds were singing to each other in the bush-tops. 'I am tired,' said sweet gentle vivacious Maraed. 'So am I.' 'Let us sit down on the moss-covered rock.' 'Certainly.' Maraed dozed off to sleep with the murmuring of the waterfall. 'Croon wind, through the trees in the swamp. Don't blow noisily or threateningly!' The wind blew gently through the sleeping wanderer's hair and laid bare her neck as white as the swan on the lake. Her little lips were as red as the rowan and as sweet as honey. Her breasts like two snow-clad knolls rose and fell like the swell on the King's River. Her neat little buttocks and her pretty little legs were hidden by her satin dress, down to her small tidy feet. Two snipe flew off from a pool near us like arrows from a bow. My beautiful young lady started from her sound sleep. 'May there be no pool for you in Ireland ever again,' said I. 'May there not be.' 'The sun is setting. Let us be off home.' We went off, tired and weary, her arm in mine, her head on my shoulder, her eyes lowered to the ground. I never remember a more pleasant day.

25th . . . I went with Pádraig Ó Sealbhaigh, the merchant, to Gráig Amhlaoibh to look at his farm. We saw eight donkeys spreading manure for one person. Donkeys are now more numerous around Callan and all over the bog than horses, although I remember the time when donkeys were so scarce that a horse would take fright at seeing one.

A farmer called Maolala, from near Callan, paid sixty pounds for a Spanish jack two years ago. He gets six pounds for a service.

30th . . . Calm warm morning. Light clouds all over the sky. Mist everywhere. The robin, my own bird[4], singing to its mate, welcoming to-morrow, sunny May-day, the anniversary of the day I, Amhlaoibh Ó Súilleabháin, was born. Wrens, thrushes, blackbirds, house-sparrows, yellow-hammers, stone-chats, meadow-pippits, larks, and

4. A reference to the occurrence of the robin on the O'Sullivan arms.

a hundred other birds are all singing together, and making love to each other, enjoying themselves in the air. One can't say that 'the song and chattering of the birds has ceased'. It is a beautiful morning, thank God. I saw flies for the first time this evening. I haven't heard the cuckoo yet.

May 5th . . . South-westerly wind since four o'clock this morning. Mist and showers till seven. Heavy clouds trailing their dark grey dripping draggle-tails over the flat tops of the low hills and the peaks of the high hills and the mountains. At mid-day giant clouds were trussing up their dripping draggle-tails and storing the sky's water in their trains. It's clearing up. Bright patches followed by dark ones with a west wind. At sunset the sky resembled a blue plain half-full of small light clouds like horned rams, fine sheep, fat wethers and pretty lambs lying beside their mother . . .

13th . . . There is sad news on Suirside. A poor hungry crowd tried to take meal from the boats which were sailing from Clonmel to Carrick-on-Suir, but the peelers fired on them from the boats. Three of the poor Irishmen were killed and six others very badly wounded. This happened on last Thursday, the tenth of this month.[5]

I went with Tomás Ó Ceallaigh and Seán Ó Mathúna, the son of Tadhg an Chúinne, down by the river to Callan

5. This incident was reported as follows in *The Freeman's Journal* (16/5/27): 'About four o'clock on Thursday Evening as four boats laden with flour; the property of Mr. Malcomson, were on their way from Clonmel to Waterford, they were stopped at Kilsheelan Bridge by an immense multitude. An attack had been apprehended on the part of the owner of the flour, and five policemen were sent down as a guard with the boats. The mob which amounted to about 1,000 persons were warned not to attack the boats, on which one of them called out "it was better to die by a bullet than by hunger . . ."

The Police at first fired over the heads of the mob, but finding that did not deter them, they were obliged to fire in amongst the vast multitude. Several persons were immediately seen to drop and upon the third volley being fired the people retired . . .'

Mills in Millstreet and to Poll Sheáin as far as the Iron Mills which was working iron some years ago. There is an iron spa beside the road without cover or shelter from the road-dust. There used to be another iron mill near Tobar na mBráthar which also burnt the country's forests, in order to prevent the rapparees from hiding in them. These rapparees were poor Irishmen who were plundered by James I, King of England, by Oliver Cromwell and by William of Orange. They used to fight with *ropairí* or short spears, and it was from the word *ropaire* that they got their name.

Some of the English themselves became rapparees and set to robbing the poor Catholics whom they had already plundered.

14th ... At the Crossroads I drank a good drop of whiskey in pleasant company. I know the Crossroads a long time, because, having come from Killarney in Kerry to Waterford in 1789, and from Waterford to Callan in March 1790, and having spent the summer in Baile Ruairí, beside Cill Mogeanna, in an orchard, I came with my father, Donncha Ó Súilleabháin, schoolmaster, to a sheep fold owned by Séamas Builtéar, between the Crossroads and Baile Uaitéir where he stayed until a schoolhouse was built for him at the Crossroads in the summer of 1791. It was certainly a small school cabin, for it wasn't more than ten feet wide and about twenty feet long.

The sod walls were built in one day. The rafters and roof-timbers were put up the next day, and the roof was put on the third day. It was many a long year myself and my father spent teaching school in this cabin, and in another slightly bigger sod-walled cabin at the Tree in Cill Dá Lua; and in a good schoolhouse in Baile Uí Chaoimh, near Cnoc na Carraige. But alas! my father has gone, and the school cabins have gone. There is no trace of their sod walls today, nor any mention of them. But what is the use of complaining? The lime-washed castles, the bright mansions, the four elements and the whole world will pass away like the smoke from a wisp of straw.

Will it be long until this Irish language in which I am writing will disappear? Fine big schools are being built daily to teach this new language, the English of England. But alas! Nobody is taking any interest in the fine subtle Irish language, apart from mean Swaddlers who try to lure the Irish to join their new cursed religion.

29th ... We struck the county rate for Éamonn Mac Craith, the Chief Constable of Callan and its barony at one shilling and a penny farthing an acre, and a heavy rate on houses in Callan. This rate is very heavy. It isn't half as much on the land in any other barony in the country.

June 15th . . . A pleasant warm heavy morning. The birds singing noisily. I saw a little girl who suffers from an illness called *aos teannta* (I don't know how to spell it properly). She was injured on St. Stephen's Day 1825, in the Brothers' Chapel in Callan, the day when fourteen people were killed, between young and old, and a hundred people injured, although no damage was done to the chapel. The people took fright for some strange reason. The little girl's back is bent, and she suffers from shortness of breath . . .

23rd . . . A fine dark calm day. Wind from the west. I went back to Cúirt an Fhaoitigh, and came home along by the river as far as Tobar Cuineach beside Balla an Eidhneáin . . . There I found lesser spearwort with a yellow five-sepalled, five-petalled flower, white bog-cotton, water-mint and the stinging nettle. The youths and young maidens are dancing about the bonfire.

24th . . . St. John's Day, Sunday. Fine calm dark day till nightfall.

The youths and young women of the town out strolling

and amusing themselves on the Fair Green at twilight. A quiet fresh night ...

25th ... A mild day, like a beautiful gentle maiden on her wedding day. Bright spells and dark spells. First blossoms on the wheat. Many meadows out around the town are being mowed.

The view from the Big Moate at six o'clock in the evening reminded me of heaven. The evening is so mild, without too much heat or cold that one could go naked, but for a sense of decency.

The boys were playing hurley on the Fair Green.

27th ... We were distributing yellow meal to-day at three halfpence a pot.

The Irishmen's spirit is greatly broken. Hunger.

28th ... I saw two water wagtails hopping and flitting within a yard of a cat which was crossing the road. They were noisily mocking the cat, which kept glancing from one side to the other at them. The poor man does the same to the tyrant when he gets an opportunity — just as the birds do to the cat.

29th ... Feast of St. Peter and Paul. A holiday ... Hurling on the Fair Green. It was a good game. The sticks were being brandished like swords. Hurling is a war-like game. The west side won the first match and the east the second. You could hear the sticks striking the ball from one end of the Green to the other. I was watching from the top-end myself with Doctor Céitinn and two priests. The well-to-do young men and women were strolling up and down on the Green and on the level causeway in the centre.

'Hurling on the Fair Green ... Hurling is a warlike game'. (p. 25)

July 12th ... Doctor Céitinn and I walked right across the bog, with Poll na Cailli west of us and Poll an Chapaill to the east, as far as Mocklers where we had a slice of baker's bread with butter and a strong drop of whiskey. We walked over the bog collecting wild plants: water-mint, bog-cotton, common selfheal (a small coarse plant with a purple head or flower), common milfoil, which has a thousand petals and a brown stalk.

We saw a lovely girl kneading wet turf. She had slender firm feet, calves and knees as white as bog-cotton, rounded fair thighs which were bare almost to her plump buttocks. Her father was once a well-off farmer, but the difficulties of life caught up with him. He lost everything. The landlord took his crops. The tithe-collector took away the table, the pot and the bed with him, and they all drove him out to wander the roads, himself, his wife and his handsome young children. That is why he ended up in a small cabin at the foot of the mountain, and why his beautiful daughter was now kneading turf pulp.

A thousand young girls and boys dancing to music on top of Móin Rua (a high platform in the middle of Poll an Chapaill). The reddish-brown hillock was shaking under their nimble feet. They are having a fine life — if it doesn't end in begging.

I can see how turf grows. There is a plant called *súsán,* a kind of moss, growing in bog-holes, which when it withers, turns into pulp. This pulp fills the bog-holes in time, and so creates a new bank of turf.

If the *súsán* has not completely withered, it is cut with a breast turf-spade, but if it has, it is cut with a winged turf-spade. It is spread on the bank to dry. But this is not the best turf. The best is that which, after it has been shovelled up out of the hole onto the bank, is kneaded by the feet and then made into sods with the hands by women . . .

16th . . . I see in a book on the Irish language by Séamas Scurry that the Annals of Donegal (or the Annals of Tighearnach), the Annals of Ulster, the Annals of Inisfallen, and the Annals of Boyle or of Connacht have been translated from Irish into Latin by Charles O'Connor, D.D., and have been printed by order of the Marquis of Buckingham.

I am delighted with this, as are the very few Irishmen who read their own sweet subtle mother tongue.

19th . . . I went to Power's of the River at Gráig Ros Ó Néana to-day. Dr. Céitinn and myself and Father Croíoch started off from the top of the Fair Green and went to the Abha Bheag River, and to Crann (or Bile) Bachaill at Cuailleach where Mac Cormaic's land begins.

It is a very fine farm. It has a farm house, a barn, a shed, etc., and a fine herb-garden in a pleasant dell surrounded by sheltering trees and a quick-hedge. It is good land for sheep and grass. Gráig is as good. It is great for milch cows, and has plenty of shelter from quick-hedges and trees of all sorts, including ash, oak, pine, alder (the leaves of which are used for dying), and spindle-trees, etc. There is also a rich sheltered orchard there. Sruthán na Glóire Stream is on the southern limit of the Gráig Ros Ó Néana land. There was once a mill on the stream, beside Cnocán an tSionnaigh, but not a stone upon a stone of it is to be seen now. The mill-pool is a dry hollow. I found some pink-blossomed centuary and water hare-hound in the meadows. Bees' nests are rare now.

We got a good meal from Power, rich smoked bacon, white cabbage, fine potatoes, and punch. We came home cheerfully and leisurely.

21st ... There is now no difference between a copper sixpenny bit and a silver one, but up to the 5th of January 1826 the silver bit was worth sixpence halfpenny. Similarly the piece of eight fourpences is only worth a half-crown exactly now. And the thirteenpenny bit is just worth a shilling, that is twelvepence. It's the same with every other coin. And the fivepenny bit, the tenpenny bit, the Irish half-crown or the thirtypenny bit, and the six shilling bit have all gone. There is not one to be seen in circulation. They would only be accepted now at half their value.

August 9th ... The sun shining brightly very early in the morning. From eight o'clock on it was dark, but fine. A mist in the evening.

I went with Dr. Céitinn through Gráig Amhlaoibh by the Large Oak and Coill an Tiarna to Doirín to see Pádraig Ó Donnchú's daughter who has brain fever. We came home by the Riasc and the Pools, and through the land at Sceach an Chloithreáin. I saw a little wheat being cut.

We saw Mac Eochaidh, the *súgán* maker's cabin at Liontán. Alas! Mac Eochaidh is walking the roads. His cabin is empty. His trade is finished since the foreign horse-collar has replaced the Irish one during the last twenty years. This is how the Irish one used to be made.

A straw rope was twisted into an O-shape, and briar withes were then woven together and put on the front of it. This was then put over the horse's head when he would be going to work. And a harness would be tied on then, by means of a loop on top and a breast-band underneath.

16th ... Two shillings and a glass of whiskey and their meals are the wages of reapers, and one and fourpence the wages of women binders. By mid-day reapers were to be had at a shilling or ninepence and binders at eightpence.

At ten o'clock this morning my mother, Máire Ní Bhuachalla Ní Shúilleabháin, wife of Donncha Ó Súilleabháin, my father, died having received Extreme Unction, by the grace of Almighty God. She was close to eighty years of age. Her husband, my father, died in the year of Christ 1808, the year of the big snow. He was buried in Cill Bhríde, beside Áth an Iúir a mile from Callan, although his family's burial place is Iríolach Monastery at Mucros beside Loch Léin in Killarney, Co. Kerry. But the pressures of life sent us a long way from our people, sixteen and twenty years ago ...

Small boys and girls are coming home with little bundles of gleanings.

17th ... A fine autumn day. Wind from the north. While I was digging my mother's grave my mind was troubled by many sad thoughts. The bones of my brother who died thirty-one years ago in 1796 were there mingled with those of my father who died nineteen years ago in 1808, and with those of my three children, two of them called Anastáisín and the third Amhlaoibh. Who knows how soon I myself will be there with them. My mother was buried at a quarter past [   ].

27th ... To-day I saw some purple loosestrife growing in a crock without any earth, but embedded in moss. I thought it very strange.

In the house of the person who grew the loosestrife

there was a young thrush's nest, with a solitary egg in it. The thrush had been going out every day and bringing in a wisp of hay in her beak, having dipped it in a drain near the house. She built a round and cosy nest in the pantry, where she could get scraps and crumbs of bread. When she found herself with a comfortable coat of feathers and when her wings had grown strong she flew out around the orchard, and never returned to the little nest nor to her single egg. And she should not be blamed for that, for every living creature loves freedom. She was perfectly right not to bring up her young brood in captivity. She did no injustice to those from whom she escaped, as they had taken her from her mother's nest in the bushes where she had both shelter and freedom.

30th . . . The corn stacks are being brought home to the haggards and being built into ricks. Some few people are piling up the sheaves in the barns. From the pile of sheaves a layer consisting of twenty sheaves is taken (two *áireamhs*, each containing ten sheaves) and from each *áireamh* a stone of wheat is threshed, if the corn is good. That is a barrel from twenty *áireamhs*, or from ten layers. A man can thresh thirty *áireamhs* a day, that is a barrel and a half.

September 16th . . . Pattern Sunday in Grange. My son Amhlaoibhín put his little foot into a pot of boiling water on his way to bed. He is roaring and crying. I have put a potato plaster on it.

18th . . . I put sweet oil and a bread and boiled milk plaster on Amhlaoibhín's foot.

23rd . . . Sceach Pattern-day (that is Sceach na Cuntaoise, the Countess's Bush), which takes place on the Sunday before Michaelmas Day.

24th . . . A wonderful story is going round the country

now. Eilineora Ní Dhorchaí, daughter of Séamas Ó Dorchaí from Baile Laighean was coming home from Cill Bhaoithín after Mass on Sunday the second day of this month, accompanied by Nioclás Tóibín and others, when she saw the fairy host around Machaire Mór. A dark person came out from the host and tried to injure her. She began to run around Nioclás Tóibín to escape from being hurt. But that did her little good, and she would have been hurt and injured but for the fact that her mother (who had died six years previously) came to save her. The mother looked sad and lonely.

The fairy host then left her, and Nioclás Tóibín and the others took her home. She was unable to speak until the cocks crowed after midnight, when she recovered her speech, but then lost the use of her leg which was as cold as ice. She remained like that for thirteen days (that is until Saturday the fifteenth of this month). She was weeping and grieving until her mother came to her and asked her did she want to be cured. She replied that she did.

'I would have come to you sooner only that I couldn't while there was anybody with you. Now that you are alone, I will cure you. Come out with me now on the road.'

They both went out, but not by the same way, and her mother showed her a herb and told her to pluck it herself, as nobody else should do it for her. She plucked it, and it had no skin, no leaves nor any flower. Her mother instructed her to boil it in water and to rub it to her leg six times, in the name of the Father, the Son and the Holy Ghost. Her mother then left her, and she did as instructed. The first time she made the Sign of the Cross on her leg, it straightened out and it is sound and healthy ever since.

It is a wonderful story, unless she has been subject to illusions, as one with fever might be, or unless it was pretence and invention on her part. But some of the neighbours say her leg was as cold as ice. It was her own father who told me the story from start to finish, and Donncha Ó Briain from Droichead Bhaile Laighean told it the same way. But indeed the latter was afraid that it was all an invention, and that she pretended that she was speechless and lame, but on the other hand he admits that reliable people told him that her leg was frozen as I said. I wash my hands of it.

30th . . . A fine quiet day. Sunny morning. I saw a web made by little spiders spread over the green grass on the Fair Green rath. Each of these little spiders is only about the size of a pin-head. When I stood above the web I couldn't see it, it was so fine, but I could see the little spiders which appear to me to be walking on air. When I looked slantwise at it, and the sun shining on it, it looked like silver gauze.

October 9th . . . Rent, taxes, tithes, county rates and church rates are all too high, and they have to remain so as long as the Royal Debt remains, that is the English Debt, the debt which King William placed on the Kingdom for the purpose of encouraging the foreign religion and destroying the Catholic faith. It was only about a million and a half at first but it is over nine hundred million now.

This is a mill-stone around the neck of the Kingdom, tied by the tyrant's iron chain. The rich collect thirty million pounds a year profit from the people of the country. I don't know how many millions are spent on the up-keep of soldiers and peelers to keep the people quiet (but not happy), under the heavy load of this debt, together with all the rents, taxes, tithes, county and church rates.

Perhaps, reader, you are not aware of how this English debt weighs down on the people in general. I will tell you about it.

In order to collect this money, every little thing must be taxed, for example, snuff, tobacco (bad luck to it), tea, sugar, whiskey, and all spirits, beer, malt, hops, iron, timber, spices, and imported goods in general, etc. etc. The tax increases the price of these items, and in that way forces the people who use them such as farmers, merchants, traders, etc. to increase the price of their food and goods.

To sum up, the wealth of the country is going to those who benefit by this English Debt, and to the support of soldiers and peelers, as I have already said . . .

14th . . . Fine soft showers before day-break. A soft warm morning. Cloudy and clear spells. This is indeed the 'Little Michaelmas Summer'.

Goats are in heat. They are fourteen weeks pregnant before they give birth to the kids. Towards November day the buck gives up, and says 'Home, if I'm able. Home, if I'm able,' when he is so weary that he can only just drag his legs along.

31st . . . Two men dug eleven barrels of potatoes for me, from morning until three o'clock in the afternoon, out of six *áireamhs* (320 yards) of poor moorland in Molaise belonging to Éamainn Mac Craith. A shilling a man to dig, eightpence a woman to pick.

November 10th . . . Tomás Ó Luanaigh, a medical student, and myself started off from the Fair Green, and went to Droichead na nGabhar, by the weir at Muileann Uí Bhriain, to the pleasant glen beside Cill Bhriocáin Mills. The sky in the west after sunset was a beautiful sight from the Mill Hill. The clouds were glorious beyond description; some scarlet, some purple, edged with gold; part of the sky green. Sliabh na mBan was hidden by heavy black clouds, like a dark oakwood. The river was blood-red from the reflection of the sky.

We came home by Mionnán Road as darkness was falling, and drank a drop of whiskey. Ó Luanaigh is a pleasant young fellow. I was with him and other good

company in Ó Ceallachán's tavern the night before last.
We were happy singing and cheering, when Doctor
Builtéar came upon us like a warlike cat would come on
lively mice chewing cheese, at which moment we all sat
down without a word.

'Go home!' said Doctor Builtéar to Ó Luanaigh.

'Yes,' said Ó Luanaigh, bending his knee and bowing
his head, his hand to the tattered brim of his hat which
was hanging down over his face (there was a tatter
hanging at each side of his face).

'I don't know what knowledge of medicine you will
have when your term is up, if you carry on like this.'

We broke up.

25th . . . I haven't been out for the last fortnight during
daytime, but during the night I used to go strolling on the
Fair Green along by the ditches down as far as the Abha
Bheag river, like the owl — the bird of the night and the
high skies. The reason for my staying indoors during the
day was one black eye, and another blacker one I got
from Dr. Builtéar on Sunday night the 12th day of this
month, or perhaps it was Monday morning, after
midnight.

This is how it happened. I was drinking with a pleasant
group in Maraed Comartún's. We were drinking hot
whiskies and sugar in plenty. Tomás Ó Ceallaigh, a
merchant, caught hold of Seán Forastal, a medical
student, and started to wrestle with him. Tomás Ó
Luanaigh, another medical student, thought it was a 'fight
of fallen-out friends' and struck Ó Ceallaigh a blow in the
face and floored him. Ó Ceallaigh jumped up, and since
he didn't know who had hit him, he started to thrash out
at everybody within reach, and gave a good smack to
Seán Ó hAithiarainn, a young gentleman, who gave a
right beating in return, and left him with a black patch on
his weasel-eye.

Then Mícheál Ó Meantáin, the 'scrip-scrape man' or
fiddler, took off his coat and joined in the fray, so that we

were all like the wild boar in the pigsty as in the story
Bruidhean Bheag na hAlmhuine.

At long last gentle Maraeidín and myself managed to
make peace between these sturdy warriors.

'Och, my dear, you've got two black eyes,' said
Maraeidín to Tomás Ó Ceallaigh.

'I am more like you then,' said Ó Ceallaigh, 'for the
ripe sloe is no blacker than your two eyes under your
lashes and dark eyebrows, and the blackbird singing on
May-day is not more melodious than your sweet red-
lipped mouth — and now that I am close to you, give me
a gentle sweet kiss!' And with that he gave her a loud kiss
that sounded like the slap of a wet tattered shoe on the
bottom of a hot pot.

With that we left Ó Ceallaigh, courting gentle
Maraeidín. We went off to Sinclair's tavern. Sinclair is an
ex-soldier from Poll Tóna an Diabhail in the north-east of
Scotland. He is not a Scottish Gael, but a descendant of
the English. Ó Meantáin started playing his 'scrip-scrape'
fiddle. Seán Ó hAithiarainn and the rest of them started
dancing wildly. Aimhlios who is like a swallow on a
branch with his two short bandy legs joins in with them.
We were dancing away happily until suddenly the angry
Builtéar darts in among us with his blackthorn raised in
one hand and his other turning up the rim of his hat, a
devilish grimace on his face, and a warlike light in his
eyes.

'When the cat is away, the mice are at play,' says he.
And with that Ó Luanaigh and Forastal run off out
behind his back; Ó hAithiarainn darts into the ash corner,
another gets behind the coal heap. Aimhlios keeps on
dancing and Ó Meantáin keeps on playing. I remain, fool
that I am, sitting on a form.

'Take away your fiddle! Don't wake up the hatching
geese. Put your playing board in your bag and your bag
on your back.'

'Indeed I will not,' says Aimhlios.

'You must do it,' said Builtéar, 'and it's no misnomer to

call you Aimhlios,[6] for you have neither *lios* nor *ráth* nor land now, although you formerly had, you grey-faced cursed little drunkard.'

'You are no different!' says Aimhlios, 'you are blind drunk!'

At that the frenzied Builtéar grabbed Aimhlios by the beard and hair and pulled him to the floor. Aimhlios himself wasn't idle. He caught Builtéar by the legs and brought him down into the slops of beer and whiskey which were spilt over the floor and they started pulling and tearing at each other like two mad dogs before they were separated. No sooner was the frenzied Builtéar on his feet again than he ran towards Ó Meantáin who was crouched up in the ash-corner and dragged him by the back of his head out onto the dirty floor and they set to punching each other in the sides, the faces and the eyes and kicking each other in the shins so that they were bruised, battered and torn before they could be separated.

Then Builtéar took one look at me as I sat there on the form, attacked me like a wolf attacks a lamb, or a hawk a lark, struck me straight in the face before I could put up my defence, and left me with a black eye. I fell back immediately, like a cow struck dead. That didn't satisfy the madman, he fell down in a heap on top of me, and gave me a blow in the other eye.

'Beat every inch of him,' said the woman of the house, a swarthy stinking, paunchy, yellow-loined, heavy-bottomed, flatfooted ale-wife, with breasts like an old cow's udder, thick shrivelled lips, flat turned-up nose, teeth like tobacco cloves, red bleary eyes, heavy eyebrows and thick serous lashes. 'Strike every soft and every hard bit of him that his mother ever laid a finger on,' said this devil in woman's shape. But with the help of friends I managed to slip away from the madman and get home, weak and weary. And 'by my buttocks,' as Giolla an

6. A play on the name which could be roughly translated as 'Landless'.

Amaráin said, 'I'll not go to the tavern for a year from that day.'

And that is how I happened to get a black eye which kept me imprisoned for a fortnight, without seeing a fresh or withered leaf, without hearing the murmur of the streams, the sound of the waves, the bellowing of oxen, or the whispering of the winter wind in the trees.

December 4th . . . In the evening I went for a walk along the Abha Bheag river up to Cill Mhinic. I collected some corn camomile, yellow ragweed, dandelion and dwarf-elder berries. The mossy moorland is not covered with grass. I plucked some puff-balls. They are so dry that they become like a puff of smoke when squeezed. They would make a perfect couch for the princess of the fairies.

On my way home as darkness was falling, the sky was angry-looking, with black, red and russet clouds. A gale was blowing from the west. I wonder was it the princess of the fairies who caused the storm, and the angry appearance of the sky, because I interfered with the moss of her bed and the puff-balls of her couch.

8th . . . During the last few days I have seen wild geese high up in the air, flocks of starlings on the grasslands and snipe in flocks rising up from the marshes.

'This is fine land for partridges,' said the gentleman to his tenant farmer. 'It is not, by your leave,' said the tenant farmer, 'but it is fine land for snipe' — that is, it is not land to grow corn, but wet marshy land.

12th . . . I got a new overcoat today — a good thing, as it was overdue. The old one was torn and patched, although I am a retail merchant . . .

20th . . . I spent a good part of the early night with sweet-voiced Maraeidín de Barra. She was singing songs to Irish tunes for me . . .

25th . . . Christmas Day. Fine and calm at dawn. Purple and golden clouds in the south-east. At sunrise golden, dark yellow and grey clouds like light fleeces, high in the air.

I see on the north side of the ditch at Clós an Chrosa, beside O'Brien's Mills, the yellow primrose, a flower which normally doesn't blossom until March. But this Christmas is so mild and soft that it is not surprising to find a number of flowers alive and budding. Although the proverb says *Every weather is like summer until Christmas,* the wild mustard, the yellow ragweed, the dandelion and the corn camomile, are plentiful. The haws and dog-rose hips and the black berries of the [   ] are still there. The blackberries have all gone. The crimson spindle-tree (the Christmas orange) is still blooming near St. James' Well.

I have roasted goose with potato stuffing for dinner, thank God for it. May God grant us a good and happy Christmas.

26th . . . St. Stephen's Day .i. the day of the wren in the hollybush. This day two years ago (1825) fourteen people were killed in the Brothers' Chapel on Sráid an Mhuilinn, and another hundred were badly injured or bruised. It was a terrible and tumultous day in Callan.

29th . . . A fine warm morning. A south-east wind which thawed the frost and broke the ice. *A puff of wind from the south is warmer than the fire at the world's hub.* At dawn there were clouds of many colours in the south-east, crimson, yellow, pale yellow, dark yellow, and grey.

The larks are going in flocks about the fields and the open plains searching for food. The house-sparrows and the yellow-hammers are high up in the bushes around the haggards. The snipe are under the withered iris and the fresh rushes in the pools. It is great weather for fowling. The hen and cock blackbirds are whispering in the ditch. I can see no thrushes. The robin red-breast is singing sweetly . . .

30th . . . At peep of day the happy twittering of the house-sparrows from the belfry and in the old castle across the way are to be heard. The robin red-breast is welcoming with them the first glimmer of day. At dawn the horizon in the east is yellowish green, and the canopy of the high heavens is clear blue. Thin clouds coloured yellow, red, crimson, russet and brownish red lie along the horizon. A grey cap on Sliabh na mBan at sunrise. At sunrise, the sun, that is the eye of the elemental world and of the planets, appears in all her glory with the heavenly bodies about her.

A thousand million times more glorious is He who created her and the whole world — his own infinite house, and every spirit both good and evil that exists.

I have pig's trotters and rich bacon for my dinner. No better dish.

31st . . . There are many words in Irish to describe the falling of moisture, for example, *drúcht* (dew), *ceobhrán* or *ceobhraon* (drizzle), *mionfhearthainn* (drizzle), *meánfhearthainn* ('medium' rain), *mórfhearthainn* (heavy rain), *báisteach* (downpour) *clagairneach* (pelting rain, the heaviest of rain). Wet weather is called *doineann* and very wet weather which would cause flooding is called *doirteadh díleanna* . . .

Now that December is over there is no more shooting of grouse or pheasant. Partridges can still be killed, although they are not easily found now. There are still plenty of plovers about. Now is the time for the wild duck. Next month, that is January, is a good month for hunting the hare, the deer and the fox. The water is too yellow and muddied for fly-fishing. The partridge flocks are breaking up now. The hen and cock are coupling. I haven't seen any flock of starlings recently. The larks are grouping together now, and so are the sparrows.

'Dr. Céitinn, Seán Ó hAithiarainn and myself went to Dún Laoire, six miles from Dublin, on a covered car, for fourpence each.' (p. 46)

DIARY 1828

Ó Súilleabháin's diary for the year of Christ, one thousand eight hundred and twenty-eight.

January 4th ... Cross is sowing bere; and crows, starlings, house-sparrows, yellow-hammers and water wagtails are flocking around him trying to get a grain of seed. They well deserve it, for it's many the worm and grub which would otherwise ruin the seeds in the ground but for the fact that these birds eat them up.

This is the season for parties. There is not a farmer who has not plenty of pork, mutton, beef or fowl, and the beggars get scraps from them.

5th ... Some of the townspeople are organising a circulating library for a limited number of members. It has been established for the last year. Every member of the society pays five shillings a year. Alas! Who will establish an Irish language library? No such person is available. The English language of the Saxons is every day getting the upper hand of our own native language. Add to that a thousand million other blemishes and deficiencies under which we are suffering since the day the English once got hold of our native land — poor persecuted Ireland.

7th ... My sister's son, Séamas Ó Coistigín married Grant's daughter from Cúlalonga near the top of the Fair Green this evening. Father Séamas Hennebry, the parish priest, married them. We spent until three in the morning eating, and drinking hot punch and tea, and singing Irish songs. We came home happily and peacefully, without causing trouble to anyone. A poor fellow called Donncha was stretched out in a cart on his way home from Clonmel. He was almost dead from the downpour of rain on his head and body, and perhaps he had a drop taken. We laid him out near the fire, and took off his boots and stockings. After an hour or two he was happy, out of danger of death, thank God, and sitting up by the fire. His knee was injured by falling under the wheel of a cart at Nine Mile House.

8th . . . The people of Callan are about to send a petition to the British Parliament, asking for Catholic Emancipation without any ties, without any restrictions with regard to religion, and without surrendering any powers we already have. They are also asking that the act against the landlords' agents be rescinded, and that the act with regard to church cess should be changed, and also that freedom be given to the English Protestants.[7]

11th . . . It is snowing heavily at three o'clock. I hear the wind murmuring at the window like a pooka trying to be let into my house, but he won't be allowed in, if the heat of a coal fire and the warmth of food keeps him out . . . The rabble in the streets are throwing snowballs at each other and annoying respectable people. I went along the Abha Bheag river with the Callan fowlers. They were shooting snipe, grey plovers, blackbirds (hens and cocks), thrushes, etc. The lapwing is not worth shooting. The snipe are by the streams in the rushes and irises. There are two types of snipe, the common snipe and the jack-snipe, which is smaller. The grey plover is a beautiful big bird. They perch in flocks on the commons around Callan. It is a brindled bird with little yellow spots . . . A grey plover is better than three snipe or even four. I saw people digging stubble today.

12th . . . I see people digging stubble land. They dig it well for fourteen shillings an acre. It would cost as much to plough it. Digging is better than ploughing, as the digging turns over the land better, cuts it more finely, and leaves no furrow or headland unturned. I read that many

7. This petition is reported in *The Freeman's Journal,* 5/1/28.

people in England are now digging the stubble. It provides work for poor people. And of course a Christian is better than a horse.

Cabbage is withering and getting dearer because of the frost and snow, although we had very little of either. We will have turnips instead of it.

We have a big market for coal, culm and potatoes today. Coal at tenpence a hundredweight, culm at a shilling or sixteen pence a barrel; potatoes at three halfpence a stone.

13th . . . We had a meeting today in the parish chapel to send a petition to the Parliament of the Three Kingdoms seeking emancipation for Catholics. God alone knows whether it will be granted now or ever. A dry quiet moonless night.

15th . . . Wheat at twenty-five shillings in Clonmel. I remember it at four pounds a barrel. At that time a boorish small farmer would swear, 'By this silver on my whip and by the spurs on my boots.' But now they say, 'By my straw-filled boots and this stick, boys . . .'

20th . . . A fine morning, as warm as an April day. Flocks of noisy starlings in the trees at Cúirt an Fhaoitigh. I see the snowdrop bowing its head like a shy pretty girl. Its white compact calyx and the corona each have three lobes. It belongs to the hexandrous class and to the monogynous order. The monthly rose is beautiful with its fruit like a little orange-coloured pear or hip, and that is what it is.

31st . . . The last day of winter .i. St. Brigid's Eve. A beautiful fresh sunny day. A gentle wind two points south of west. This last day of winter put on a pleasant appearance as if it were saying, 'I was soft and easy with you for the last three months, and now, as we are going to part let us shake hands with each other in a friendly manner. Good-bye!'

St. Brigid's Eve, that is the evening and night before St. Brigid's Day. The little girls are going from door to door with *brídeogs* (images of St. Brigid dressed up in lovely clothes), asking for halfpennies — and getting them — to have a party for themselves, just as the young boys do with the wren in the holly branch on St. Stephen's Day.

February 1st . . . Fair St. Brigid's Day, the first day of spring. A beautiful fresh sunny day, without cloud or fog in the sky, with a gentle south-westerly wind until a quarter to four, when suddenly, like a shot, a storm arose that shook the house from top to bottom. It brought with it hard hailstones. This sudden blast lasted only five minutes, and it was well for the Callan people that it didn't last longer, for I never heard the likes before except for one particular storm. After the storm the sky cleared up quickly. A quiet moonlight night with light clouds . . .

A fine month for hunting the fox and the deer. The best month for hunting the hare with hounds. For the young hare is too weak in September, and she will be with young in March. But during this month the hares are mating and if you come on a buck in a furrow, you will find a doe in the next one. Partridges should not be shot this month, but one can go after the snipe, the woodcock and the grey plover. *Every second day is fine and beautiful from St. Brigid's Day till St. Patrick's Day.*

3rd . . . I went to Cuailleach to start collecting the Catholic Rent there.

Myself and Pádraig de Búrc are the two Wardens of Charity of this Callan parish, and we have to collect the Catholic Rent each month for Councillor O'Connell and the Catholic Association.

There is a lonely path near Uisce Diúin and Móinteán na Cisi which is called the Mass Boreen. The name comes from the time when the Catholic Church was persecuted in Ireland, and Mass had to be said in woods and on moors, on wattled places in bogs, and in caves. But as the proverb says, *It is better to look forward with one eye than to look backwards with two* ...

7th ... The white willow has budded well. Pelting rain early in the morning. After the downpour, the morning was fine and sunny with thin clouds.
⟨ I hear that it is the cock lark that sings up in the air, and the hen on the ground. I see and hear the redwing. It is about the same size as the thrush but not as neatly shaped. It has only a short call. The wren and the 'wren's boy' *(buachaill an dreoilín*[8]) are happily flitting through the bushes. I see the grey wagtail in the double ditch on Talamh na Mionnán beside the river. There is iron and iron water across from Oileán na Giúise and the Iron Mills. There is a well of iron water beside the mill on the south side of the river ...
The well-off people, men and women, are strolling about the Fair Green late in the evening. Frogs are now busy spawning.

10th ... In Cuailleach collecting the Catholic Rent. Got a great drenching coming home. The birds were sad and silent. The Mass Boreen, Móinteán na Cisí, and the Mass Hollow, where Mass used to be said during the persecution of priests and of Catholics in general, are lonely places. A moonless windy showery night.

11th ... I hear no bird singing. There are many names for the song of the birds: the birds' *ceiliúr*, the blackbird's *scoighaire*, the cock's *glao*, the hen's *grágadaíl* or *grágallach* or *grágaíl*, the crow's *grág*, the cuckoo's *cuachaireacht*.

20th ... Ash Wednesday. *Drinking milk on Ash Wednesday is a great temptation.* Milkfoods are not eaten

8. Unidentified bird.

today. I had bread and porridge for dinner. A fine sunny
morning; wind six points south of east.

21st . . . We have 'cobbledy' for dinner today. It is not
right to call it *cál ceannann* (white-topped kale) for there
is neither kale nor white cabbage in it, but white potatoes,
fresh milk, good salted butter, salt as well, and pepper and
onions warming it up. Myself, my children and my poor
dear wife are gobbling it up — we have plenty of it, but
not too much.

March 9th . . . Dr. Céitinn, Seán Ó hAithiarainn and
myself went to Dún Laoire, six miles from Dublin, on a
covered car, for fourpence each. A sunny day, wind from
the south, dust on the roads. A marvellous large harbour
is being built there for the protection of ships which will
come in there during stormy weather.

16th . . . I was invited to dinner to Fr. Uilliam Grás's in
Baile Uí Chaoláin. He is a great talker and a great lover
of his country.

17th . . . St. Patrick's Day. A fine dark calm day. The
people are happy drinking their Patrick's Pot. Shamrock
in every old hat or caroline; and every girl with a cross
. . .

April 3rd . . . Tenebrae was sung melodiously by my
brother Donncha Ó Súilleabháin, and by Fr. Eoin de Rís,
and other psalm singers in the Brothers' Chapel. This is
now a very beautiful chapel. The wimbles and other roof
timbers have been covered with ornate work in plaster of
Paris, and also the walls.

4th . . . I wasted a lot of time during last month with a law
case between Dr. Céitinn and the apothecary, swarthy
Cróinín . . . Two thatched houses in Little Bridge Street
were burnt down about mid-day. It is well it didn't happen

at night . . . Tenebrae was sung by the choristers in the Brothers' Chapel.

5th . . . The water wagtail's whistle is a short one, just like the sparrow's. I can see and hear a flock of birds flying past in the air, but I don't know what they are. They are the same size as the snipe. There are three types of sparrow, the house sparrow, the yellow sparrow (yellowhammer), and the hedge sparrow. I see the *éinín-cois-bo*[9] which is the same colour as the lark but smaller. The bunting has a sweet little song. I can see no snipe now. I hear they have gone off to Móin Éile and other wild places. The wild duck were driven off from Desart Court a month ago by firing guns, so that they wouldn't lay and hatch there, because if they did, the young ducks would die of hunger owing to their great numbers.

The oats are being sown rapidly. It's a good thing that they weren't sown unknownst to me. I wasted time with other people's law case. But a stand must be made against the English no matter how difficult it may be to make it.

6th . . . Easter Sunday. *Easter Sunday and Christmas Day are the two best days for eating.* I had chicken and smoked ham for my dinner to-day.

I found a small bird to-day called *Seán an Chaipín* or the reed-bunting.[10] It is smaller than the sparrow, dark russet, with a black head, a spotted black breast, a greywhite belly, and a dirty white band around its neck, from beak to beak. The inner feathers are the colour of the slates in Áth na Slinnteacha . . .

Boys were playing hurley near Droichead na nGabhar in the evening. The sticks and the hips were busy, when Fr. Croíoch came and chased away the hurlers. They ran before him like a flock of sheep before a lion. We came home laughing gaily and talking noisily . . .

9. Unidentified.

10. Ó Súilleabháin himself gives the English as 'black-cap', but his detailed description would suggest it was a reed-bunting.

*'The sticks and the hips were busy when
Fr. Croíoch came and chased away the
hurlers'. (p. 47)*

30th . . . I hear the young boys had two golden May-balls
in the fields to-day. They got them from two newly-
married couples last Shrovetide. They have a May-bush
on top of a stick or long pole, with the golden ball in the
middle of it, and they dance around it with the young
girls.

There hasn't been a May-ball in Callan since 1782,

when Seán na Sál killed Butler.[11]

A quantity of straw is lighted at each side of a gap and the cattle are driven through the fires. This is an old custom handed down from the days of the Pagan gods.

May 5th . . . Flora, my little bitch, has been in heat this last week. I'll know how long it will be before she has a litter.

11th . . . The people of the Commonage got a letter from. Alexander Dawson, member of Parliament for County Louth, and another from Lord Duncannon, informing them that the bill that was against them in Parliament to impose a rent on their cabins and gardens or else to cast them out in the world to beg, steal or murder, has been thrown out. A thousand thanks to God, the devils have been defeated. Our Parish Priest, Father Séamas Hennebry, Dr. Céitinn, myself and others were of good assistance in the affair.

16th . . . There are many things connected with ploughing, for example, the plough itself and its various parts, namely the sock, coulter, foot-tie (a short chain), handle, two small swingle-trees, and a large one, the ploughman and the two horses, and the tackle, that is the headstall, the straw collar, harness, chains, and back-band for each horse. I remember when four horses were used to draw the plough, and corresponding tackle and a driver with a long chain. I remember six horses ploughing summer fallow with two drivers, each with a long pole with iron goads on it and a *ceann bata* or a boy with a forked stick in his two hands keeping the sock from rising

11. 'Tuesday, a number of people in different parties assembled at Callan in order to collect may-balls, they disagreeing, a quarrel immediately ensued in which Nicholas Butler of that town, cooper, unfortunately received a blow of a stone in the forehead and instantly expired. The offender has since fled'. *(Finn's Leinster Journal,* May 1st-4th, 1782).

up out of the ground. It's many a *hob!* a *hó!* and a *hó-ar-ais!* these four called to this ploughteam and *'hob, blackie! 'easy there brindled garrán!'* etc., while they gave a painful prod to the poor horses in the side and a blow of the pole on the back. And it was many a cry and shout of 'The devil take your body' from the ploughman to the two drivers and the *ceann bata,* and it was many a sweet sad song the four used to sing to humour this team of six.

17th . . . I read in the paper (The Kilkenny Independent) that the Russian forces crossed the Pruth, one of the rivers that divide Russia and Turkey on the 26th or 27th of April. As a result I suppose war will soon flare up. The French have a fleet in Toulon ready to sail to somewhere in Turkey (or in Greece to my mind), and the High King or Emperor of Germany has a large army on the Danube, which will probably not remain idle.

The greedy Englishman is in a quandary, like a man 'between the cliff and pirate' not knowing whether war or peace would best suit him.

The Catholic Question (an unsolved question) is being debated in the House of Commons in London. I don't know what is going to be the end of this difficult question.

26th . . . Whit Monday. Ballingarry Fair Day or Cill Baoithín Fair, the most vicious fair in Munster or in Leinster. For there is many a devilish blackguard with a stealthy stick, many a yeoman, tricky lout, and large-headed rogue with a white knobbed ashplant cracking senseless skulls and brainless mindless mannerless heads.

There's many a swarthy old witch
firing stones,
both large and sharp
from streets and walls,
making pigs go mad,

cows crazy,
bulls bellow,
and sheep bleat.

There's many a tent being invaded,
And pipes being played,
Beer being ordered,
And ever-flowing punch,
Being served to maidens.

There's many a ragged nag,
Mare in foal,
Long-tailed colt
And stallion neighing,
And goats a-bleating.

Men are drunk,
And women senseless,
And the mob in the street
Are shouting and laughing.

The tinker's wife,
With her ugly snotty child,
Has quantities of ginger bread,
While her man incites the rams.

There's many a smeared butcher
With red mutton;
And pots on the boil
And leather bellows.

There's many a pack-man,
And ugly vagrant,
And snotty child,
Without even a rag on it,
Screaming and screeching
At fine young women,
Who are being cuddled and kissed

By handsome young men,
Joking and dancing
On smooth green lawns,
To the music of bagpipers
And of scraping fiddlers.

There's many a proud maiden
And strapping boastful fellow
Calling for drink in taverns,
While the ale-wife
Welcomes and serves them
The maddening whiskey,
The juice of the barley
Which will set them crazy,
Both young and old,
While they have a penny in their pockets,
Or the 'shilling-purse'
Swishing on their hips.

There goes Siobhán off home
On the nag's rump —
Pillion rider to her friend
Tabóid of the songs,
After drinking their cups,
And they without even a shell
Nor a second pot,
Only a few sticks of furniture
At home in their hovel.

After the night's carousing,
The Farrelly family
Have bodies bruised,
Hats broken,
And breeches torn,
Filthy boots,
And dirty stockings,
Ragged jackets,
Buttonless vests,

Tattered shirts,
Blood-stained faces,
Not a farthing left,
Not even their pack,
Tramping the muddy boreens
And dikes of water
To their wretched hovel
Beside Abha Mhuimhneach.

There's not a nook or cranny,
Nor corner of headland
Nor path by Abha Mhuimhneach,
From top to bottom,
Where they haven't pitched a tent
Or made a hut.
The wagtail itself
Can't shelter its head
Or build its nest,
They have all been chased
By the Mac Lóbais clan
The vampless-stocking wearers.

27th . . . I remember the time, about thirty-five years ago when every able-bodied farmer used to sow peas and beans. The potatoes took their place. Very few people, apart from the gentry, cultivate them now . . .

June 9th . . . The thing they call 'cuckoo-spittle' is to be seen on sorrel and many other plants. The poets and writers on natural history say that it isn't the spittle of the cuckoo. There's an old phrase in Irish, 'it's not worth the cuckoo's spittle,' which is said in reference to a useless thing.

20th . . . I had a meal in Fr. Séamas Hennebry's house. We had two fine sweet solid trout, one of which was the size of a small salmon, and hard-boiled hen eggs, boiled asparagus dipped in butter melted in hot milk, with salt.

We had port, hot punch (as good as I ever drank), and of course, it was not to throw stones at it we put it in the jug!

23rd ... St. John's Eve. I see a poor hedgehog being tortured by the street rabble. Although its body is prickly its actions are harmless ... Many St. John's Torches to be seen on hills and mountains around about, although there is no good bonfire in Callan. This is unusual.

I don't see many people on their way to Achadh or to John the Baptist's Well.

29th ... Little St. John's Day. Fair Day in Thomastown. Feast Day of St. Peter and St. Paul, apostles ... Cherries and red and black currants for sale at Crois. A sultry day. Hurling on the Fair Green. I was knocked down by a young brat, but it was nothing to be ashamed of, as I brought him down as well. *Cow-dung often knocked down a good man.* Everything is now growing as fast as ferns.

30th ... I see a woman with a handful of common selfheal. All she has to do with it is to put the complete plant — stem, leaves and flower — into cold fresh water and stir it until it produces a froth like soap suds, and then give it to someone suffering from 'the small fever'.

I went for a walk with Risteard Ó Loinsigh, a retail merchant, to Abha Bheag, Baile Mailearta, Cúirt na Buaile, na Bánta Buí and home again. There is a very fine quarry on the border between Baile Mailearta and Cúirt na Buaile. Lime is produced there, and tomb-stones are cut there by Pádraig Ó Sé, stone-mason. Cúirt na Buaile is a thickly wooded townland. There was once a Court there, as the cut stones are still to be found in Ó Briain's dairy-yard.

Good rain for four hours ...

July 8th ... Every window in the town was full of lighted candles in honour of Daniel O'Connell who was elected in County Clare as member of the London Parliament.

10th . . . St. John's Fair Day. Good trade in cattle. The devilish peelers beat a lot of innocent people. They beat up two merchants in their own houses. They can't be tolerated.

13th . . . I went with Seán Ó Riain from Sráid an Mhuilinn to Baile Nua Chapel to collect the Catholic Rent.

Lapwings are crying near us. The lapwing is a cute bird. She lures me away from her nest with her noisy chattering. Here is a verse about it:

'Lapwing where do you have your nest?'
'I have it down in the hawthorn hedge'.
'I'll go down and rob it'.
'Oh, do not, there are two eggs in it'.

But the lapwing never builds her nest in a hedgerow, but in the meadow and in the bogs.

I was one of the jury of twelve that held a coroner's inquest in the evening on Ó Meachair from Cnoc na Rátha near Cill Mhanach, who was killed by two peelers at St. John's Fair in Callan, on the tenth of this month of July.

We found, after sitting for five hours that it was by the two above-mentioned that he was killed. Great barley is ripe on the Cill Bhriocáin lands.

16th . . . I put a handful of white hoarhound in boiling water and gave it to a young girl from Carrick-on-Suir as a cure for a hard cough. It often cured myself.

18th . . . I see swifts flying around in circles, catching flies in the downpour of rain. It is on flies that they live. I didn't think flies would be so high up in the air until I saw the swifts hunting them a hundred feet up.

I went to Kilkenny to prosecute swarthy Cronin . . . I went there and returned in Céitinn's widow's car for one and eightpence. Seven of us had dinner in Rose Inn. We had salmon and fresh hake and new potatoes, bread, beer and punch. It cost us three shillings a head.

20th . . . A great fire on Cnoc na gCapall Hill above Bearna na Gaoithe in honour of Daniel O'Connell and the Dalcassian voters.

22nd . . . I had dinner with the parish priest, Fr. Séamas Hennebry. We had boiled leg of mutton and a roast bird with spiced stuffing. We had punch, tea, and songs in Irish till ten o'clock.

31st . . . I went to Kilkenny in Céitinn's car. I was trying to get the peelers prosecuted who killed Mícheál Ó Meachair on Callan Fair Day, the tenth of this month.

August 5th . . . One of the peelers was acquitted by trickery. The other, named Ó hIcí, was found guilty of manslaughter. I don't know yet what the sentence will be.

8th . . . I bought striped and yellow calico from a travelling trader at fourpence a yard for six-finger wide cloth, and fourpence halfpenny for seven-finger wide cloth. I get sixpence a pound discount for ready cash . . .

13th . . . The wheat-stacks are going up quickly now. The Tipperary reapers are coming into the county, into our own lovely valley of silver and corn, that is County Kilkenny or Lower Ossory.

15th . . . Hundreds of spalpeens and women binders were engaged towards. night. Tomorrow will be a busy day, a Saturday between two holidays in the Autumn.

16th . . . Nineteen pence and a glass of whiskey is being paid to sickle reapers; and some were getting two shillings at day-break. Not a reaper could be got for any money after that . . .

18th . . . I can hear no bird sing. They are all ill because they are getting new feathers. Birds begin to grow new feathers at the beginning of this month, but they don't have a full coat of new down and feathers until the middle of September. Many of them remain sick and weak afterwards throughout the winter until spring arrives. The weaklings die while the new feathers are growing. I don't see any birds yet. Are they all dead? I hear not the cackle of the crow, the voice of the eager blackbird, the call of the cheerful thrush, the song of the lark, the chirp of the robin, the note of the wren, the cu-cu of the cuckoo, the ack-ack of the corncrake, the 'fuid-fuide' of the quail, nor the song of the grey linnet. The fieldfare is not happy, nor is the weak-legged swallow. I don't hear either the house-sparrow, the yellow hammer or the hedge-sparrow. The wild pigeon is cooing in Inis na Giúise, beside the weir at O'Brien's Mill. 'The melody and chattering of the birds is silent' *(Tá siansa is gliadar na n-éan go ciúin)*[12] . . .

September 2nd . . . I went to the Abha Bheag river which is being deepened. There is a wooden bridge at Áth Mhic Óda since last week. Limestone as black and smooth as the stones in the black quarry in Kilkenny is being quarried there to the depth of six feet. They are five hundredweight and under. They are round stones. An odd coal stone, and some culm and black slate are to be found near them at the same depth in the subsoil or the marl. There is sand within a chain's length of them, on the same land down by the river.

It couldn't be a Fianna cooking place, for if it was, the

12. A line from O'Rahilly's poem *Marbhna Dhiarmada Uí Laoghaire na Cillíneach.*

slate would not be black; and especially because the place called *Droim an Ghuail* (The Coal Ridge) is within six miles of it, at Lios na mBroc, Cill Náile, in Baile Liam. There is coal in Baile Uí Chaoláin also, but it is not mined.

A few days ago a dog was incited to attack a sow in farrow. When she produced the litter, two of the piglets died, and nine of them had the shivers. They can't suck the teat if they don't keep it in their mouth all through the day and night.

3rd . . . The seed is being blown from the thistle. The thistles are being cut by the paupers for fuel. I see a load of them, as big as a pigsty being carried on her back by a poor woman. They use dried cow-dung for fuel as well.

4th . . . A quiet misty dewy morning. There are many field-spiders' webs hanging from the branches in the ditches. And there are many dew-drops in each web. This is how the web is. Numerous radii stretch from the centre to the circumference, and these are woven together by numerous strands, like the woof through the warp. The common spider is a hundred times the size of the field-spider. The latter can hardly be seen by the eye without a microscope — nor can the web on which the dew drops are, except by looking along the grass on a warm summer's day . . .

14th . . . Sunday. The Cuailleach pattern day, that is the Sunday after the Feast of Mary. A fine dry sunny day with few clouds. A fresh lively wind from the north. Tomás Ó Niuláin saved his barley. He had many women binding it and men stacking it.

Four of us had a meal with Fr. Séamas Hennebry. We had boiled leg of lamb, carrots and turnips, roast goose with green peas and stuffing, a dish of tripe boiled in fresh milk, port and punch, and tea. We also had melodious songs in Irish, and spent a merry night till eleven o'clock in peace and good cheer.

22nd . . . A delightful soft cloudy day. 'No puff of wind to stir a tree-top or flower' *(Gan gal ann den ghaoith do chroithfeadh barr crainn ná bláth).*[13] People going off to the coalmines in the early night, at nine o'clock. People getting themselves ready to go to Cill Bhaoithín or Ballingarry on Sunday with green banners and green dress to bring about reconciliation among the Gaels. May God grant that the Protestants won't finally oppose these meetings. There were meetings in Fethard, in Cashel and in many other places since Daniel O'Connell opposed Vesey Fitzgerald in County Clare.

26th . . . It is a sad night for Pádraig Deibhriús's family. He was killed today by a bullet or bullets at Cluan Uí Gheara, near Poll an Chapaill bog, where he took a farm of about forty acres, which had been occupied by more than five families whom he evicted from their cabins two months ago.

I was there on the twenty-second of August last. Having gone for a walk along the Abha Bheag river, I decided to come back a more direct and easier way. I went to a miserable cabin, on the edge of the bog, to ask the way. A poor tall thin ragged barefooted woman came out to me. Her hair was black and tousled, with no cap or fillet, her eyes were red, and she was weeping bitterly. She had no clothes to her back except some rags discoloured by soot. 'Where is the short-cut to Callan?' I asked. 'I'll show you that and welcome,' said the poor woman. 'Let us go through the potato garden by the path near the hedge. It was I set these potatoes, but it is Pádraig Deibhriús who will dig them.' As we went through a field of wheat, she said 'It was my family who sowed the seed, but it was Pádraig Deibhriús who reaped the crop, my curse on him!' Going through the yard, she said 'These wood-pigeons were mine, but it will be in Pádraig Deibhriús's pot that they will be boiled. It was my

13. A line from Seán Ó Coileáin's poem *Machnamh an Duine Dhoilíosaigh.*

husband who built that house. It was I who put soot on the rafters, but the son of Páidín na gCeann (Páidín of the Heads) took the door off the jamb, and the hinges off the hooks. He left the cabin without a door, the window without a pane of glass, the hearth without a fire, the chimney without smoke, the pigsty without sow, boar or bonham, big or small, fat or thin. I'll never again hear my cow low to her calf or to her yearling, my mare neigh to her foal or to her colt, my sheep bleat to her lamb, my goat meg to her kid, my hen cackle to her chicks or pullets, nor my cock crow. I won't be here to see again either my white duck or my spotted drake, my hatching goose or my fair gander. I won't see the bog lake. I'll hear no more the heron's or the wild goose's cry, the lapwing's or the plover's call, nor the jacksnipe's bleat. I won't see the cormorant again. I won't hear the plopping of the water-hen. I won't drain the pool to catch an eel or a pike. It is far from them all I myself, my poor persecuted husband and my ruined children are being sent by the man who murdered Pog Ní tSeafra. I won't be here to grow sweet white-topped watermint in the meadow by the pool, nor the white or red clover in my dry meadow. I won't set the flax-seed. I'll not cut the flax. I'll not steep it in the pool. I'll not draw a thread from my spinning wheel or my distaff. I'll make no more yarn. My spinning wheel for flax and wool is in the ditch, my press is in the sandpit, my table on the fence, my pot in the undergrowth, my chair out in the rain, my straw bed has no cover, sheet or mattress, my head no cap, my back no cover or cloak. The back-rent collector has taken them all, alas!'

27th ... A coroner's jury of twelve, with two justices, held an inquest on the death of Deibhriús today. It appears that his skull was broken by an axe, and that his brains were dashed out. Shots were being fired in the same neighbourhood, but they were being fired by people who were shooting partridges. It is not yet known who killed him, but the people who were evicted from their houses are suspect.

The heron perches in a tree at night. Her quiet call is not unmelodious, although her loud cry is sharp.

It is a sad sight to see Pádraig Deibhriús laid out on a layer of straw, covered by a sheet.

28th . . . Sunday. Early this morning O'Connell's League of Peace people were being encouraged to beat their drums and gather together and depart for a meeting with the County Tipperary League of Peace. The Scully and Funchion families from our side will be there. They are all dressed up in ornate ribbons, green, yellow, red, white, blue, purple, brown, scarlet, dark red, every colour under the sun except orange.

It is following O'Connell's advice that this reconciliation and peace is being brought about among the Irish. But the English don't like it, as they think it is easier to defeat quarrelling parties than friendly people, and that is true. But I don't like to see — neither do other responsible people — women and children, and drummers and musicians with banners, for example, ones with a picture of O'Connell, etc. on them because that will incite King William's followers, that is, the Orangemen, against us.

Pádraig Deibhriús was buried at four o'clock in the afternoon. I spent the evening and some of the night at Fr. Séamas Hennebry's the parish priest's house. We had three dishes, tripes done in milk and butter, bacon with beef kidney and white cabbage, and roast duck with green peas. We had punch and songs until ten at night.

A custom common in Munster in my time,
A group of people in one house would gather,
To hear fairy music, lays, talk and poetry,
And one person only paid for all their drink.

There is a heronry on the banks of the Suir between

Carrick-on-Suir and Waterford. They don't breed in the pools or on the bogs, as I thought.

29th ... The sixty-sixth regiment of infantry has arrived. Their band was fine.

October 2nd ... We are plagued with soldiers coming through the town today — some of the eighty-sixth infantry regiment, unarmed, on their way to reinforce the rest of the regiment who are in the West Indies ...

4th ... I have been very busy this past week trying to persuade O'Connell's followers not to march in green clothes nor with O'Connell's image, nor with music. The Catholics of Callan have promised not to march any more. The Protestants pretend that they are very frightened, but they would be delighted in their hearts to be spilling the Catholics' blood.

There was a fight between the peelers and the O'Connellites at Baile an Chaisleáin near Nenagh. A barrack was burnt. Con Ó Néill, from Clogheen, a supporter of Emancipation, was sent to prison to Clonmel. This is the beginning of trouble unless the Catholics stop in time. I hope to Almighty God that they will, and that they won't make their mortal enemies happy, namely the Protestants and the devils.

5th ... A showery day. A strong south western wind till four in the afternoon. The Seventh Light Cavalry Regiment went through the town today on its way to Clonmel. They are doing two days' journey in one day in order to be there in time. But I hope to God they will not be needed there.

From four o'clock on, the day was calm and sunny with blue skies. We had a fine meal at the parish priest's. We were seven merry men and one young woman. We had a leg of lamb, bacon, pullets and white cabbage, two roast ducks and green peas; white wine and port, and plenty of punch till eleven.

10th . . . Friday, Michaelmas Fair Day. Dark clouds on the mountains, mist on the hills, and a fresh south wind in the early morning.

Fógraim féirín ort or *m'fhéirín ort* ('you owe me a fair-day gift') being said by everybody. I see a lot of hornless cattle at the fair. The proverb that says *Don't buy a hornless cow, don't sell a hornless cow, and never be without a hornless cow* is not being observed, for they are now being bought and sold.

I bought two castrated male slips for three pounds, eleven and sixpence, and paid fourpence custom. A great variety of articles, livestock and fowl for sale at the fair, for example, horses, cattle, sheep, pigs, turkeys, geese, ducks, hens, cocks, pullets, chicks, onions, apples, wooden and delph ware, flax, wool, and small goods. A good price was got for everything, especially for cattle and fat sheep.

No rows took place, and not a blow was struck by man, woman or boy at the fair.

11th . . . Saturday. St. Stafán of the Fair's Day. A sunny thin-clouded morning. I went, on the priest's mare, with Mícheál Ó hAithiarainn, senior, to Butler Clerke in Newtown to ask him to sign the Protestant Declaration, in favour of Catholic Emancipation. He signed, as did Henry Baker, junior, from Cill Cobhráin, and Arthur Bushe, the son of the Chief Justice.

I must get the name of every Protestant in the parish on it, if I can.

Isn't it a sad thing to see the children of the Gael seeking freedom as an alms in their own native land. But they themselves are responsible for being kept in slavery by English foreigners, because of their own failure to agree among themselves since the time of Brian Boru up to the recent O'Connell Peace Movement.

The end of the day was showery with a south west wind. A large number of workers sowing wheat with spades and shovels. A few groups digging potatoes. A shilling a day is the labourer's pay. It's not bad pay for the short day at this time of the year.

18th ... Although this is good weather for work and
business, I am lonely when I no longer hear the voice of
the cuckoo from the drooping branch nor the ack-ack of
the corncrake in the nettles, nor the *fuide-fuide* of quail in
the field, nor the song of the blackbird in the whitethorn,
nor the call of the thrush from the shady branch, nor the
warbling of the female blackbird in the briars, nor the song
of the lark high up in the air, nor the sweet voice of the
linnet in the ring-fort. But the chirping robin didn't leave
me, nor did the brown wren, when the busy swallow
departed.

26th ... A very fine meal at the parish priest's house.
Maraeidín de Barra sang for us there.

27th ... The parish priest, myself and Tomás Ó
Flanagáin went to Cnoc an Tóchair to encourage the
commons-dwellers there, as we already encouraged those
in Callan to oppose the tyrants of this country, who are
about to take the commonage from them ...

28th ... A calm dark dry day. People digging potatoes.
A slight north east wind. Four cannons passed through
the town. But, thank God, Leith Mogha (the southern
half of the country) has never been so peaceful. So there is
no need to use these big guns against the Irish in the
south. The Ulster Protestants and the Protestants in
England, namely the Brunswickers, are mad, like
bloodhounds, to devour the Catholics.

November 2nd ... Yesterday was the last day of the
Kilkenny horse races. They were on for only four days.
Although the venue of the races was packed with people,
not a blow was struck, nor was anyone heard saying
'you're lying'. A stand had been erected and a large
number of tents were serving food and drink. We had

trick-of-the-loop men, thimble-riggers, rafflers, wheel-of-fortune men, lucky dips, jugglers, and a hundred other tricks not worth mentioning.

6th ... Raining in the morning with a strong south east wind. Every dike needs to be drained, as they are brim-full from yesterday's rain, and last night's and this morning's. This is the time of year when the English commit suicide, according to the French fiction that in the gloomy month of November Englishmen hang and drown and shoot themselves.

11th ... St. Martin's Day. Millers don't turn any wheel today. Nor would a spinner turn her wheel, nor a ploughman put his team to work. No work involving the turning of a wheel is done. I don't know the reason for this, if there is any reason.[14]

I was at a wedding yesterday. I am thirsty today. *Long as the drinking may last, it always ends in thirst.*

25th ... Master Richard Corr commenced learning of my son Denis, Nov. 19th, 1828, being Wednesday.

A poor bull — I pity him — is being baited these last two days by the wretched street rabble and by the dogs of the town.[15] They are a mad cowardly crowd ...

27th ... I went for a walk to Cill Bhríde at Áth an Iúir. I walked from the Áth an Iúir Bridge along the Abha Bheag river through Cill Mhinic Commonage. The boreens between the poor hovels in the Commonage are dirty and muddy. In spite of their wretched condition Lord Cliften,

14. It was generally believed that St. Martin was killed between mill wheels, and for that reason it was not right to put any wheels working on his feast-day.

15. Bull-baiting was carried on under the auspices of the Kilkenny Corporation in the Bull Ring, up to the 19th century. According to Prim (*Transactions of Kilkenny Archaeological Soc.*, II 326), bull-baiting was held for the last time on Sept. 29th, 1837.

and the other landlords and gentry are trying to levy a
rent on them. May they not succeed in their plan! Amen.

December 4th . . . A delightful blue-skied soft fresh and
sunny day. A mild south west wind. Cnoc na Carraige
and Cnoc na Rátha hills with their pine groves are
delightful. Desart Court with its dark oak woods is
delightful. The mountains and the landscape are
delightful. The people, the cattle, the birds of the air and
the fish of the river are delightful. Every aspect of nature
is delightful, since the Creator caused the sun to shine on
us, in spite of our wickedness.

A quiet moonless night. November with its moonless
nights is considered a good time to sow wheat.

5th . . . There are many ways of naming the wind, for
example (i) from the point from which it is blowing .i.
north wind, west wind, south wind, east wind, north east
wind, north west wind, south east wind, south west wind;
(ii) from its strength or weakness, for example, *siolla
gaoithe*, a very light wind; *gal gaoithe*, or *sonnadh*, a puff
of wind; *anfa*, a storm; *guairdeán gaoithe, sián gaoithe, sí
gaoithe*, a whirlwind; *rabharta na Féil Michíl i.e.
ruaghaoth*, the Michaelmas equinoctial wind, a blasting
wind; *gailbhe, gailbhín* or *gaillinge*, a storm with clouds;
gaillshionn, gaillshionnach; gairbhshíon, gairgshín, a
tempest; *gaorsta, eachan gaoithe*, a whirlwind.

*All weathers up to Christmas are like summer, and no
cold until St. Brigid's Day* or *All weathers up to
Christmas are like Summer and a storm on St. Brigid's
Day* says the proverb.

18th . . . The potter's kiln-house on Moat Lane was burnt
down at nine o'clock at night. The flames from the kiln
caught the roof, which was thatched. It was well it
happened during the wet weather or else every house out
in Little Bridge Street would have burnt out.

There's not a house or cabin left standing in Moat

Lane now, for Hanraí Ó Riain, Lord Cliften's rent-collector levelled them all, six months ago, and sent the cabin-dwellers wandering the roads. The potter's kiln-house was my school-house about [   ] years ago. I had one hundred and thirty scholars there at all stages from learning the alphabet up to fluxions.

24th . . . Wednesday. Christmas Eve, a fast day. A thin-clouded morning. A mild south west wind. A blue-skied day, as fine as May-day. The poor people are buying pork

The town rabble going from door to door with a wren in a holly bush . . . (p. 68)

chops, pigs' heads, soggy beef, big joints of old sows'
loins, and small bits of old rams, as all the good meat has
been already bought up by the well-off, well-fed people.
He who comes last will be the loser, as usual . . .

25th . . . Christmas Day. Before daybreak the moon was
shining in a clear sky without cloud or mist, welcoming
the good Infant Jesus. A big drum being beaten at five
o'clock. Fifes and clarinets being played by the youth of
the town.

26th . . . St. Stephen's Day. It is difficult to go hunting
with a pack of hounds today, for it is extemely hard for
the hunters to follow them, the country is so wet. Snow on
Sliabh na mBan Fionn from the bottom to the top of Suí
Finn, that is, the peak of Sliabh na mBan.

The town rabble going from door to door with a wren
in a holly bush, asking for money so that they can be
drunk tonight. It is a bad habit to give it to them. Few
people at Mass in Callan today because of the wet
morning. It was very different three years ago today,
when fourteen people were killed at the Brothers' Chapel,
and a hundred injured. It was a dreadful affair.

DIARY 1829

January 15th ... I started writing Ó Súilleabháin's Diary on the first of April, 1826, but God alone knows when I'll finish it.[16] I am Amhlaoibh Ó Súilleabháin from Loch Léin of the delightful islands and the pleasant airy grassland surroundings. I am now living in Callan of the Ructions in the County of Kilkenny ...

The starlings and the fieldfares fly about together in groups, although they are not of the same colour or kind, nor have they the same cry. People behave differently — two different classes or races mix very badly. Light rain from twilight till dawn.

18th ... Black frost this morning. A quiet sharp north east wind. A dark cloudy windy day. At the Parish Church the people are signing an appeal to Parliament for Catholic Emancipation. Snow at nine. Rain for most of the rest of the night.

21st ... A delightful fresh sunny day with a clear sky. Hard frost. Ice one inch thick. People sliding on pools. Slight south east breeze. *Frost is better than continual rain*. Birds are being caught in traps, made with a small loop, a fork, and a 'treacherous stick'. A small grain of corn is used to tempt them into the trap. It is easy to take advantage of the severe and horrid hunger.

22nd ... Black frost today. Ice an inch and a half thick ...

At four o'clock I see great smoke belching from the house of some small farmer near Baile an tSagairt. I see a mass of flames at sunset about five o'clock. It is a sad ending to the day for this farmer and his family being

16. There is no evidence for this date. The diary proper does not begin until the first of April 1827, although it has a few brief entries for the period Jan.-March 1827.

burnt out of their house on such a bitter night — a boisterous windy starry clear-skied night.

26th . . . The snow is melting fast, although it is still on every hill and mountain, and in every ditch and dike.

I heard a thrush in a cage singing early this morning for joy, now that the frost and snow are melting. She hasn't sung since this frost came. The sparrows are chattering noisily as well. They can now get food. They can happily say 'Here's out with hunger', like the housewives say on Little Christmas Eve 'Here's out with hunger from tonight till this night next year and tonight itself', as they throw a loaf of bread against the door.

February 27th . . . Maraed St. John came to me today to work for seven shillings a quarter . . .

March 17th . . . Patrick's Day. A holiday. Pelting rain and a west wind before dawn. A little flakey snow at eight in the morning. A bright sunny day from then on. A happy group of us drank our Patrick's Pot in Fr. Séamas Hennebry's, the parish priest's house. We had fresh cod's head, salted marinated ling, smoked salmon, and fresh trout, with green cabbage and fragrant cheese with our meal. We had white wine, port, whiskey and punch in plenty . . .

April 9th . . . I hear the caged thrush singing, although I don't hear the free thrush. That shows that the wild birds have to be careful to raise their brood quietly, which the caged birds need not be. The thrush rears three broods a year, in the beginning of April, in May, and in June. She begins to build her nest in the very beginning of March in a stump of an old tree or in a hedgerow, in a place where food is easily found. She makes a deep round nest with moss or withered grass, and lines it carefully with clay. She leaves a hole in the middle at the bottom to let out

wet. At the end of March or the beginning of April, in
May, and in June the young come out.

14th ... A fine warm thin-clouded morning. A gentle
south wind. At mid-day I sheltered in the opening of a
lime-kiln at Talamh na Mionnán. Lesser celandine and
daisies are plentiful in every meadow at this time. They
will soon be all covered by the green grass. Primroses and
violets are plentiful. I can see only one hyacinth. They will
be plentiful next month along by a large hedgerow at
Talamh na Mionnán. Strawberry blossoms brighten
every hedgerow. Ground-ivy is plentiful. It smells like
mint. I see a single small flower, with a stalk about a foot
long, almost the same colour as the apple-blossom, that is
white and purple, most of it white, of the order
monogynia of the class long tetrandria and short
dyandria. I don't know its name ...
   I hear the thrush today. I believe it is starting to court
its mate again to have another brood. You must
understand that it is the cock that sings for the hen.

22nd ... A heavy cloudy day. A strong cold east wind
with light rain. Spent this day and night in Kilkenny.

24th ... Showery day. Cold north east wind. Came home
from Kilkenny at mid-day. What little business I had
there turned out badly for I spent two days drinking and
the third sick enough.

28th ... A dark dry blustery morning. A bright sunny
day, with blue-grey sky. A stormy wind from the west in
the morning and from the north-west during the day.
Slates were blown from the roofs of many houses. I see
the dark-backed brindle-bellied swallows hunting for flies,
along by the river near Poll Sheáin. I was in the same spot
a fortnight ago and I didn't see a single one there. Since
then it seems that they came from the warm far-away

countries. Pity the poor fly by the river. The fish is after it in the water, and the swallow in the air . . .

May 1st . . . Sunny May Day . . . Green blossoming branches are on the mail-coach horses coming from Dublin at half past six. The mail goes from Dublin to Cork in twenty-one hours, although it is only fifty years ago since the coach from Kilkenny to Dublin used to take two days, although Kilkenny is half-way between Dublin and Cork. At that rate that coach, called 'The Flyer', would take four days to do one day's work. 'The slow flyer' would be a more appropriate name. But the blame couldn't be put on 'The Flyer', but on the English Parliament, that left Ireland without proper travelling facilities — nothing but muddy roads and rough paths, fords without bridges, hills and rough glens, unlike the level even road, without hole or rock, steep ascent or descent, sharp bend or filthy boreen, which we now have from Dublin to Cork; and from that on to Bantry in the south, to Limerick, and thence to Killarney and south to Valentia and Dingle . . .

3rd . . . Two May-balls were taken up (that is a May-bush covered with silk, ribbons, flowers, etc., and a ball hanging down in the middle of it, also covered with ornaments), one from the Grónta family in Cúlalonga, and one from the Breatnach's on the Fair Green. The young men played hurling with one of them later. The golden apple that Paris took among the Goddesses did less harm than some of these May-balls do. Before this a May-ball hadn't been taken up since a man was killed taking a May-ball from the newly-married minister, Dr. Lampart at Callan Cross fifty years ago.

5th . . . I am teaching school now, and writing an adventure story in Irish so I have little time to go out walking.

10th . . . The whitethorn has no blossoms and the blackthorn has very few blossoms and no leaves.

I don't hear the cuckoo, but I walk very little now since I am teaching school . . . *When the cuckoo calls on a leafless tree sell your cow and buy corn.*

A fine soft pleasant nightfall with a fresh gentle breeze. Great hurling on the Fair Green.

June 12th . . . I hear the corncrake and the quail. Although these are not melodious, they are good to hear, because they come with the summer. Question: where do they spend the winter? It seems they stay here, but stay quiet. Fowlers say that we have quails here in the winter . . .

28th . . . I sat up all night with my wife who is ill. The call of the corncrake is lonely.

30th . . . My wife very ill. May Almighty God cure her. My poor children will suffer a great loss if she dies suddenly. *One's end is sleep, and a woman wakes her own corpse.* She sleeps badly. Her leg is paining her. She is failing greatly. She stayed up two or three nights a week ago, and that left her very weak. She has a bad cough. God help her . . .

A troup of actors were performing on the Fair Green. They danced, played music and performed acrobatics. A cloudy night.

July 1st . . . Raining all the morning from day-break until ten o'clock. A calm north eastern wind. Dry at mid-day. Showery at the close of day, with a lively cold north-west wind.

Now, at this moment, at eleven o'clock at night my wife died, having received Extreme Unction, by the will of God.

2nd . . . A fine thin-clouded sunny day. A mild west wind. I was never alone until this day.

3rd . . . Incessant rain up to five o'clock, with a slight north wind. I buried my wife in Uachtar Rátha. I never felt alone until the day the grave was dug. My eldest son, Donncha, is sad and sorrowing, but as regards the other three orphans, Anastás, Amhlaoibh and Séamas, they don't know their loss.

5th . . . Sunday dinner was lonely without Máire, my wife. My youngest son almost got killed today by the blow of a stone on the temple. He was struck by a child with no sense. Ill-fortune rarely comes alone.

26th . . . St. James' Day, the Pattern Day at St. James' Well near Callan. A fine sultry sunny thin-clouded windless day. *Not a puff of wind to stir a tree-top or a flower*. It is a real summer day. It was sorely needed, for yesterday and the day before were almost as cold as a day in March.

I went to the Pattern with the three youngest children. There were gooseberries, currants and cherries for the children; ginger-bread for the young girls; strong ale and maddening whiskey for those who wanted a row, and for those who tried to make the peace; open booths full of courting couples; bag-pipers and fiddlers playing music for the young people; and pious people doing the rounds at the well. I left the well with my children at six o'clock. There were respectable well-dressed crowds coming from every direction.

August 15th . . . Two men, Seán Ruiséalach and Tomás Mac Óda were condemned to death for the murder of Deibhriús. Three others are being deported for life.

I see stooks and stacks of corn.

28th . . . The hovel in which Séamas Soinseán, my maid's father, lives at the end of the Green caught fire at half past ten. It wasn't a quarter of an hour being burnt to the ground. The hen, the piglet, and the few sticks of

'Strong ale and maddening whiskey . . .
open booths full of courting couples . . .
bagpipess'. (p. 74)

furniture, that is, an old straw-bottomed chair, a handless
pot, a basin, a tub, and the pot-loop, were salvaged. The
stick of the pot-hanger, and even the pot-hanger itself,
were burnt.

31st . . . I left Callan in the evening in the Italian's car[17]
and I went to Kilkenny for one shilling and eight pence. I
stayed there until nine at night, when I took the mail
coach. The night was warm and calm, with a north wind.
At half past two in the morning a heavy fog fell which
lasted two hours. I was in Dublin at seven in the morning.

September 1st . . . Having arrived from Callan, I went to
buy goods in Duffy's Warerooms in Lower Bridge Street,
and in other houses . . .

17. Bianconi, who set up a car service in 1815, and had up to one
hundred cars carrying passengers and mail by the middle of the
century.

'I left Callan in the evening in the Italian's car'. (p. 75)

4th ... I came from Dublin to Kilkenny in eleven hours for six and sixpence on the day coach. I walked from Kilkenny to Callan at an easy pace. I was at home with my orphans at nine o'clock. A quiet night.

November 3rd ... I dug my potatoes today. They are good, and big, thank God. I brought them back home to my new house, which I've rented from Pádraig Ó Sealbhaigh for twelve pounds a year. It is twice as big as the one I had before this from Séamas Mac Úir for twelve guineas a year. They are both in Green Street.

December 10th ... Fr. Síomón Breatnach spent some time with me this morning.

12th ... Many people set corn this last month, but planting is finished now until next April ... There are many names for cattle from calf to old cow for example *lao* (young calf), *gamhain* (young heifer), *gamhain rua* (cow in calf for the first time), *athbhó* (cow in calf for the second time), *loilíoch* (cow who has been two years giving milk, but has not yet taken the bull), *foragach* (cow or *agh* which has been three years yielding milk without being in heat). *(Agh* means a cow from which *for-agh-ach* derives).

27th . . . Sunday. I left Callan after nine o'clock Mass. I got a little black horse, a good trotter, from Séamas Ó Loingsigh at Droichead na nGabhar. I passed through Cathair Leisc, crossed the Camaisc, passed Barr Scuab, went through Dún na mBogán, crossed Sruth na Glóire stream, which rises at Drom Dearg near Gráig Ros Ó Néana, and continued on by Baile Roibin at the foot of the Walsh mountains, and then to Baile Hugúin on the mountain.

At Mass time everywhere was covered with snow, the fields, the hills and the mountains, but I didn't feel it too cold until I came to Baile Roibin at the foot of the mountains, where I had a glass of malt, a half noggin for three halfpence. The road rises up to the south from Baile Hugúin and goes over one of the hills in the Walsh Mountains — for there are many hills in the range. Here I felt the cold bitterly. The tiny snowflakes were as sharp as needles. Not much snow was to be seen on the mountains, for it was so hard as it fell that it left little trace, but the ice was four inches thick here, whereas in Gleann an Rí, beside the King's River it was only two or three inches at most, where the snow fell in large soft fleecy flakes.

I kept on going over rough stony glens, bare of trees, grass or any growth except mountain reeds, red ferns, withered heather or short sharp furze. I kept on by the Móin Rua moor. There are many rough rocky hills around about it. I continued on, crossed frozen streams, passed by ice-covered lakes whose names I don't know, while the needling snow was being driven against me and my noble little steed by a piercing south-east wind, blowing over the top of Sliabh gCruinn, the highest mountain in sight.

At last I reached Mullinavat on the other side of the Blackwater, and there I found a blazing turf fire in the hearth, and a glass of whiskey to keep me alive . . . I continued along the Blackwater, which rises from Tobar na hAbha Duibhe. The Sliabh gCruinn mountain sheltered me here from the south-east wind.

The Blackwater is a rough river, for many rocks fall into it from the hills. It sweeps down with its numerous noisy streams and narrow rivulets, winding their way through wild glens.

But they are all quiet today because the frost has frozen and dried them up.

I continued on to Muileann an Bhró, a place where only a little snow had fallen during this week and the ice is thin. From this it can be concluded that the cold is more severe up in the mountains and in Gleann an Rí, along the King's River at Callan of the Ructions, than down near Waterford, where I got a hundred welcomes from Father Síomón Breatnach and his family. There was a fine meal ready for me. We had freshly salted loins of beef, white cabbage, roast goose with bread-stuffing, a leg of mutton and turnips, bacon and pullets, a roasted snipe. We had port and punch.

And there was something else there, Máire Bhreatnach, a fine tall rosy-cheeked sandy-haired lady, with her well-shaped buttocks and full firm fair breasts. She is about thirty-five. Her skin is not very fine, as it has a slight trace of small-pox, but she is quiet and well-mannered, and has an honest gentle look. She would scarcely look at me, nor let me take her fair hand in mine, as she knows I came by invitation to court her. But the affair will come to nothing.

28th ... I spent part of the day seeing Waterford City and the shipping there, and the rest of it courting fair Máire Bhreatnach. I think I managed to soften her heart, as she gave me to understand that she would come home with me. I told her many a pleasant story, as Fr. Síomón Breathnach and the widow Murphy and her two nice young daughters stayed out of the way on purpose. We have only to wait till Twelfth Day to be married. I am getting a good dowry with her, and I think she will make a good stepmother for my four orphans, for she has an easy-going friendly appearance, like her brother, Síomón the priest . . .

29th . . . After breaking my fast, I moved off homewards over the rough summits of the Walsh Mountains. A sharp north wind was blowing against me, and small snowflakes were falling hard and heavy on me.

She is a hard-earned woman, but a good thing is seldom got without paying for it.

DIARY 1830

February 5th ... A morning of hard frost. Snowflakes started to fall at one o'clock, with the bitter south-east wind. It is the coldest day I have felt this year. *No cold until St. Brigid's Day.* Snow as fine as the sand of the seashore, as hard as grain, as dry as kiln-dried oats, is being blown by the bitter wind all day and night. It is a hard night to make a journey towards the south-east. There is not the smallest hole on the windward side of a house that the continually falling snow does not penetrate.

May God look after the people in the cold fireless cabins.

14th ... A fine quiet soft dry thin-clouded morning. The banns for twenty couples were read out in the chapel today. The parish priest will get a good sum when he marries some of them, but others are poor and he will get little from them, but *bundles are made from straws and heaps from stones.*

28th ... The first Sunday of Lent ... this is *Domhnach na nDeoirín,* the Sunday of Tears — the tears of the young girls who were not married this Shrovetide ...

March 17th ... Patrick's Day ... This is a blessed Patrick's Day. I can see nobody, not a man, woman, or boy drunk, a million thanks be to God! This is the result of Fr. Tomás Ó Deabhrán's sermons, by the Grace of God through Jesus Christ.

April 2nd ... An airless morning because of an unusually heavy fall of snow in small flakes. The slates of all the high houses and the roofs of all the low cabins are covered with white. The colourless air is gloomy. The lively wintry wind coming from the heights of Scotland in the north-east is piercingly cold. *The severe winter comes into the month of May — may it swallow her up entirely* says that cold treacherous giant, for he comes like a thief in time of fog. There is no shelter, neither in wild overgrown places, nor in the prickly hedgerow. There is no shelter on the level plains or the large fields. The grey sky is like the face of an old wizened man in the throes of threatening death. Where is the yellow flower of the furze now? Hidden under an overpowering white cloak. I don't hear the sweet music of the birds singing to each other. Sad is the mooing of the cow; loud the lowing of the scraggy hungry heifer. Uh, uh! It's cold! . . .

9th . . . Good Friday . . . It is a day of black fast. The meal that they used to have in the old days on Good Friday was 'barley bread, water-cress and water' . . .

12th . . . Easter Monday. *Lá na Cúbóige* (Egg-batch Day). Boys and girls were not eating their Easter Eggs together. They hadn't their usual fun, laughing and dancing. The majority of them stayed at home, for Easter Monday is no longer a holiday. The bishops have decided it is not to be a holiday as they think that holidays are harmful in a heretical country like Ireland, and the Protestants hold markets and fairs on holidays for the express purpose of bring them into disrespect.

18th . . . Two poor spalpeens died suddenly in Callan this week. They had a miserable wake.

19th . . . The weather is very severe for emigrants to The Land of the Fish (Newfoundland), as the hard wind is directly against them. May God help them. The poor Irish have to suffer much hardship in an effort to earn an honest living in foreign countries since the foreigners came to Ireland.

20th . . . A fierce storm with the wind from the west from earliest morning. A stormy blustery morning, with a piercing wind. The wind is whistling through keyholes and under the doors of empty buildings. A bad door has a poor chance against the wind. Woe to him who has a badly pinned down roof which hasn't shelter from a hedgerow or forest.

The crew of the heaving ship is to be pitied. Seán Ó Broin, my sister Eilís's son, and Mícheál Ó hOistigin junior, my sister Síle's husband, are on the Atlantic on their way to Newfoundland. May Almighty God save them from the dangers of the sea . . .

21st . . . It is hard severe weather for the adventurers to Newfoundland. It's not joking, but in earnest I am when I say that it would be a relief to them 'to be back home again or in some port' as Donncha Rua Mac Con Mara or Giolla an Amaráin said[18] . . .

25th . . . The hatching places are loud and noisy with the sharp cries of the fledglings and the old crows. The yellow cowslip is fine in a few places. Although it is closely related to the primrose it is a hundred times less common in the fields. I don't see it at all in the hedgerows.

The town is full of the King's cavalry. I hear George the Fourth is in danger of death. May God direct his soul to the right faith, towards a good death after repenting and receiving Extreme Unction — but I have little hope of that!

May 1st . . . The mail-coach is decorated with May branches. There are fine flowers on the horses. They are a lovely sight. A shower of hailstones in the evening. I hear the corncrake 'ack-acking' and the quail 'quid-quiding'.

6th . . . I hear the cuckoo for the first time this year. On my left-hand side I heard it — but of course that is no harm. It's only nonsense to say that luck follows hearing

18. A reference to *Eachtra Ghiolla an Amaráin,* a mock-heroic poem by Donncha Rua (1715-1810) in which he describes a journey to Newfoundland.

it on the right-hand side. It is considered a severe curse to say to someone 'may you not hear the cuckoo'.

8th . . . There is a large long underground cave in Baile na Síg, two miles west of Callan, which is called the Rapparees' Hole. It seems they used to hide there after Cromwell's and King William's time. It's many the fine good honest man who had been reared in luxury and happiness who was reduced to robbery, begging or exile by those two Englishmen.

19th . . . I made my Easter confession today, with the help of Almight God.

Top-sod being burned near the Abha Bheag river.

20th . . . Ascension Thursday . . . '*A pookeen (blinkers) is a good thing on a thieving cow.* What sort of a supernatural being is a pooka? It seems they used to spend their time hiding in underground holes. Does the word *púicín* come from *púca* or from *puca* (a bag)? *Púcaí poill* (pookas of the hole), *Ráth a' Phúca* (the Rath of the Pooka) are also said.

June 23rd . . . Tomás Puirséal (from Kilkenny City) and William Conway from the county walked from Waterford Bridge to Kilkenny City for a large bet. They walked the first fourteen miles in an hour and three quarters, from Waterford Bridge to Ballyhale. They stopped for ten minutes there and having taken a little food and drink, they walked on side by side with lively agile steps to Dún Feart, where they had a small drop of whiskey and pure water. They walked fairly slowly from there to Cloch na dTrí Míle, and from there on they started to run fast, keeping up with the galloping horsemen. A large crowd went out from the city to meet them. A young brat bumped against William Conway, pushed him and knocked him down. Because of that, Tomás Puirséal got to Guilfoyle's in High Street in Kilkenny before him. Both

of them walked thirty-two English miles in four hours,
that is eight miles an hour for four hours . . .

Steam cars are travelling in England at twenty-five
miles an hour, carrying heavy loads and passengers.

There is no bonfire in Callan tonight, as a man was
killed, this time last year, at the fire. But from Cnocán an
Éithigh at the end of the Green I can see many *sop Seáin*
(John's straws) alight. There are flames on every hill and
mountain, and loud voices to be heard in every green glen
around strong fires. In County Limerick of the bare
pastures they have fires on May Eve. It is said that these
are in honour of Beal or Baal, that is, the sun. The *tine
Beal* or *Bealtaine* was lighting on *oíche Bhealtaine* (May
Eve) at Tara of the Kings when Patrick came to Ireland in
the reign of Laoghaire, King of Ireland.

25th . . . The countryside is fresh green. This rain will do
everything good — wheat, oats, barley, grass, potatoes,
fruit and vegetables — except newly-cut hay. The cows'
and horses' skins are burnt from the blasting east and
north winds that we had recently. The cows were going
dry. The pastures had a scorched appearance, but now
they will be as green as corn in the blade. New potatoes
will soon be in the crofts, and two-rowed barley in the
fields and that will bring relief to the poor — may
Almighty God help them.

The black famine is in Kilkenny and in Waterford, etc.,
that is in the large towns and cities, but in the small towns
like Callan and in the countryside, alms are to be had
more plentifully from the small farmers. The small
farmers are very good people. It is they who, almost on
their own, feed the poor people of Ireland. They get little
food from the gentry, for it is abroad in far distant lands
that that devilish crowd spend their time and the rents
which they snatch from the Irish tenants, who are being
crushed in the grips of poverty by them and their rent-
collectors. Tradesmen and shopkeepers are also generous
in giving alms to God's poor.

I see a plant like *dillisk* (dulse) which is called 'carrageen'. Many cooks put it in sweet dishes to give them more firmness . . .

26th . . . The black hunger is in Kerry. It is ninepence halfpenny for a miserable stone of potatoes there, and the workers are getting no work or pay. It will be all right, if it doesn't get as bad as the severe famine of the year twenty-two. County Clare is as bad, and Dublin is no better, as potatoes are tenpence a stone, and pay is small. In County Sligo a prize is being offered to anyone who imports oatmeal from England, oatmeal that the English acquired from Sligo already — that is 'bringing turf to the bog'.

The people along the canals are keeping food from getting to Dublin, in case the horrible famine will reach themselves. Things are severe enough here in poor Callan, but thank God, the dearest potatoes are sixpence a stone, and some of them are fivepence halfpenny, but they are not even worth that. They are worth nothing.

28th . . . Horse races begin today at Ráth Chloch, beside Dún Feart, south of Kilkenny City. I hope to God the field will be soft under the horses' hooves, although the racing people themselves do not like that. But I am more concerned with the shortage of new potatoes than with the temporary pleasures of the race-course.

29th . . . A hundred thousand people at the races. It is a pleasant sunny place.

July 1st . . . This day last year, Máire Ní Dhulachanta, my dear wife, died. I and my family should be in tears, but a dead person is no spouse for a living person. What will my four orphans do if I marry again? What will they do or what will I or my business do, if I don't. I am between two minds. May God direct me on the path best for myself and for my poor children. Amen, merciful God.

3rd . . . Father Pádraig Grace, of the Augustinians, was buried today in Cill na mBráthar, in the Friars' Monastery north of the Friars' Well. He was ninety years of age, and had lived a life of sanctity. He was an urbane pleasant virtuous person. He had been a teacher in his youth before he took holy orders. Nobody ever saw him drinking to excess. He was like an innocent child among the people. Nobody has been buried in the old graveyard for a long time since this House of God was turned into a barracks. The graveyard in which this saintly body has been laid is a lucky and blessed one. He came from a respectable family from Ceapach Éidín. They were small farmers who came from Pobal an Ghrásaigh (Grace's Parish) in the north eastern part of Co. Kilkenny.

A wonderful story is told about one of the Graces in the time of Cromwell. Cromwell asked Grace to bring food and drink to one of his camps for his redcoats. Grace said he wouldn't, that he himself had already a large enough family to feed. The tyrant Cromwell became furious, for he thought no Catholic would have the courage to refuse him. The next day Cromwell saw a crowd approaching him on white horses. 'These are enemies', said Cromwell to one of his officers, 'take some horse-soldiers and cut them down or drive them off'. No sooner had he spoken than the men on the white horses had reached him. 'Who are you?' said Cromwell. 'I am Grace', said their leader. 'This is my family, twenty-one sons and their servants, and they are enough for me to feed, without considering feeding your redcoats as well'. 'Fair enough', said Cromwell, 'where are ye going?' 'To Sunday Mass', said Grace. Cromwell didn't prevent them, although he hated the Mass, but the Graces were originally from England, and that is why they were let go free. Had they been Irish Catholics, they wouldn't have got off so well.

It was in Cromwell's time that the English soldiers began to wear red uniforms. That is why they are called 'redcoats'.

8th . . . Farmers are at many kinds of work just now, burning lime, drawing culm from *Droim an Ghuail* (the Coal Ridge) in Sliabh Ardach; re-turning the summer fallow land. Many operations have to be carried out on the land from the time one crop is cut until the next grown, for example, ploughing stubble to make summer fallow land, *goráil* (cross-ploughing), re-turning the soil, harrowing and sowing. I don't know the root of this word *goráil*. Perhaps it is from *garbháil,* for the cross-ploughing is *garbh* (rough). *'The returning is the worst'* is a proverb, which is also used in reference to people who go back on their bargain, in buying or selling.

Very dark with a few drops of rain and a sharp west wind at ten o'clock.

10th . . . Feast of St. John of the Fair, that is, St. John's old Feast-day . . . Although there was a large crowd at the fair there were no arguments or fighting.

11th . . . I only see one person half-drunk after the night. This is not as it used to be. We used to have many a travelling tinker, a bespattered spalpeen, a poor foolish lout, a sick weak brat on the dirty streets of Callan of the Ructions . . .

14th . . . *Wet is cold,*
Late is sad,
Trite is bitter,
Abstention is sweet.

That is a churlish inhospitable verse . . . The Irishman does not regard it a sad thing for his friend or a stranger to stay late in his house, nor does he think it a bitter thing for him to come often, nor does he regard it as a sweet thing for him to stay away from his house or his table.

The heavy clouds cleared at twilight.

17th . . . I slept heavily this morning. *The bed is spouse to the grave, the grave is spouse to death, the night is spouse to cold hell, it is a sad business . . .*

18th . . . I went to Kilkenny on foot. I was wearing a pair of strong new boots. They destroyed my feet. I spent the day drinking, on the spree. That is a bad habit. I had a bad bed there. There were bugs in it. I couldn't sleep a wink.

19th . . . I got home from Kilkenny at five o'clock in the morning. The sun was shining brighly through scattered clouds, the birds were singing quietly and sweetly as I walked along barefooted, because my boots are still too stiff and short for me. I will get used to them.

Three people were buried today. They died of poison, which by accident was in the soup they had. Many people are ill from the same cause. Dean Stephenson gave it to them by way of alms, but it was the bitter alms. The father, mother and child were buried together the same day in the one grave. The paupers of Ireland are in a state of despondency now. The poor smith escaped from the annual bondage which is suffered by the poor of Ireland during the hungry month of July. It wasn't he who escaped, but greedy terrifying Death snatched him away by means of bitter poison. It was well his wife and child went with him, and that they didn't stay behind in loneliness and sorrow, seeing the forge implements with no hand to use them to provide their daily bread. The music of his sledge or hammer striking red-hot iron on the anvil will never again be heard. Dark beads of perspiration will never again be seen on his cheeks. His long arm will never again hold the tongs over a fire, blown into bright flames by the large bellows, puffing and blowing, expanding and contracting in turn. His all-powerful arm will never again put a shoe on a neighing stallion, a skittish mare, a shaggy gelding, nor a lively kicking colt.

The three coffins, covered with white sheets, were side by side in a cart. Men, heads bent, were drawing the cart with ropes to the final resting place, where the smith was buried deep down on the windward side, his dear wife beside him, and the little child in her arms, as they used to lie together in their marriage bed. *The grave is akin to the bed, death is the spouse of the grave.* Och, och, this trio will have a long sleep till the day of judgement, when they will arise together beautiful and happy, with the help of God, and go to the city of Glory singing songs sweeter than any human ear has ever heard.

22nd . . . Myself and my son Donncha, a youth of sixteen years, left Callan at five in the morning in a cart, drawn by a tiny little donkey, which trotted off lightly with us to Baile Mhic Andáin (Thomastown). Páidín of the Donkey was driving, and of course he had no need to use the whip on his haunches to get him to move quickly. It was a lovely fresh morning . . .

Summer fallows are being turned a second time. It is easy to plough them down to the *fadhb,* that is, to the bottom of the top-soil. (It was from Páidín of the Donkey that I heard this word *fadhb).*

The court house when full of people on a hot day is a roasting place. My process against Seán an Chaisleáin, (Seán Mac Cormaic na Cuailli) went ahead, but the one against Éamonn na Móna Ó Meachair (Neddy of the Bogs) was adjourned for a while by trickery. It will be for a long while if Neddy of the Bogs gets his way. Although I had served a process on Neddy of the Bogs for seven pounds sixteen shillings, towards the end of the day his solicitor called a false witness to swear that I owed him three pounds, but he didn't succeed in getting him to do it.

I and my son retired to a fine feather-bed with a pair of white clean sheets, and every other comfort, but the bag-piper, Coltannach, was playing, and cursing, and wrangling with drunkards. They kept me from sleeping. I got up with my son and we went to Mangan's where we slept heavily until six in the morning.

The bagpiper . . . was playing . . . They kept me from sleeping.

23rd . . . A pleasant airy sunny morning. At seven o'clock I went down by the Nore. It is shallow now. Near the town there is a weir to catch salmon and trout. There are fragrant woods, pleasant groves, fine walks and nice houses along by the river. I can't see how a large boat or even a narrow coracle could be drawn up against the river in the fast-flowing shallows, except when the river is flooded. It would be easy enough to sail a large boat down to Inistioge, where the tide comes in, but it would be hard work to bring one against the current, for the Nore is a rough and dangerous river during a flood. I saw no boat, big or small in Thomastown, except for a few coracles. Thomastown is a small poor town. The dwelling houses are falling down. The stores are without wheat, oats, barley or flour, without butter, bacon or beef. The storehouse doors are falling off their hinges; their windows are without glass and grass is growing in their yards and porches. If the red fox came from his lair, he would find nothing to wake up in the dark empty rooms. One or two mills are grinding. There has been no prosperity in Thomastown since Waterford Bridge was built. Before that there used to be a good market in the town, and grain, meat and butter used to be sent down to Ross and Waterford by boat. But since the bridges were built, nothing is sold in Thomastown — *Baile an Chandáin, baile an chanráin* (the town of Mac Andáin, the town of complaints).[19] The only things I saw for sale there were two small churns of milk-and-water. I came home. A fine soft night.

26th ... The paupers are picking potatoes out of the edges of the ridges. The 'black famine' is in their mouths. It would be hard for God to blame them, but, on the other hand, it is a bad habit, for if the poor people start thieving in a small way there is a danger that bigger thieving and stealing, pillaging, plundering and taking by force will follow. If someone breaks one commandment however

19. The town was named after Thomas FitzAnthony Walsh, and called Baile Mhic Andáin, or Baile 'c Andáin in Irish.

small the offence may be, there is no knowing when he will stop. This month is now called Hungry July. *Buímhís* ('yellow month') is its proper name in Irish. It is a suitable name, for the fields are yellow, and also the faces of the

The paupers are picking potatoes out of the edges of the ridges. The 'black famine' is in their mouths. (p. 91)

paupers are greenish yellow from the black famine, as they live on green cabbage and poor scraps of that sort.

A fine warm day. I went swimming with my two sons, Amhlaoibhín and Séamaisín. The water in the river was warm. There were many youths bathing there.

27th ... A fine airy clear-skied sunny morning. A thin fog like washed and combed wool on the large glen, but every fair hillock, green-sided hummock, well cultivated mound, russet-topped hill, rough-sided mountain and proud projecting peak are free from any white fog or slightest cloud. My servant girl is weeding my potatoes. The commonest weeds among them are coltsfoot, thistles, cat's tail, and grass. 'Cat's tail' is not an unsuitable name for *brobh-i-dtóin,* for its top is like a cat's tail. There seems to be two kinds of *brobh-i-dtóin,* because one kind is called *brobh-i-dtóin na luachra* (bullrush cat's tail) although it is not like the bullrush.

Men on Abha Bheag road, at the end of the commonage, are working with spade, shovel or pick for ninepence a day. Others are breaking stones for threepence a day, that is, threepence a heap which makes three horse loads. This is a bad division between workmen. Muiris Read's men from Cill Mogeanna are getting ninepence, and the men from Callan commonage threepence. I will make a severe complaint about this injustice to some important person who will get justice for the Callan men.

A fine warm day. I haven't felt as warm a day since the year twenty-six. Myself and my scholars are melting with the heat. I have them separated. Half the town is out swimming.

28th ... Myself and two of the well-to-do people gave out a lot of yellow meal to the paupers of Callan, for twopence a pot. This is a great relief to them.

30th ... The food which I and my family eat is warm food, namely oatmeal porridge with milk in the morning, wheaten bread and milk at one o'clock. That is a cooling mid-day meal. Potatoes and meat, or butter, in the coolness of the evening.

The size of the heap of stones has now been reduced for the Callan men. They earn sixpence a day. It was no harm to let the wicked supervisor's treachery be known. He was getting the sweat of the men's hearts and brows, without paying for the work.

My potatoes are growing wonderfully.

August 1st . . . Plentiful full August. Sunday, the first day. A heavy-clouded morning after a quiet peaceful night of continuous rain. A south-westerly wind. This is the rain of St. John's Day, and it is more than welcome, for it is a generous welcome rain. It makes men energetic, women generous, complaining old women calm, cantankerous women placid, beautiful young fair-haired girls gentle, grey old weakly people strong, and gay young boys lively. It gives colour to the cheeks of the lovable child, and milk to the cow. All the world is now at rest, and here am I writing.

A downpour at seven o'clock.

5th . . . A lot of important people are coming home from Paris. A war is on between the King of France and his people. It is said that the King is in the wrong. It is forty-two years since a King of France was at war with his people. He lost his head then. His name was Louis the Fourteenth. This King, Charles the Tenth, should have more sense. The Parisians and the National Guard in Paris and two battalions have sided with the people, and the King's Life Guards with the King. Many were killed on both sides. I am told peace now reigns in Paris, but I am much afraid it will not last long, if the King tries to suppress their Charter of Liberty. He suppressed their newspapers. That incensed the people. May God direct him and them. War would greatly damage the Catholic religion, as it already did when thousands of priests and holy people were beheaded during that rebellious war in the reign of King Louis. The students of the universities, namely the medical students, were on the people's side. These youths are wild and excitable.

25th . . . Sickle reapers are getting only sixpence a day, and women binders fourpence. The weather is too cool to ripen the harvest quickly. As well as that, good pay is rare after a hungry summer, for the poor things accept whatever pay they are offered.

26th . . . There was an argument about religion in the Poor School between Dobbin, the Minister, and Father Seán Ó Deabhrán. Ó Deabhrán was well able for Dobbin.

28th . . . A dry cloudy day. A cool north wind. This autumn is cooler than any one I remember, apart from 1817, when we had seventeen weeks of continuous rain which rotted the ripe corn and that already cut on the ground, and left the rest unripened. I myself saw oats, still unripe, being cut on the first day of the new year in 1818, the year of the plague when thousands of people died, as a result of eating rotten half-ripe food. There used to be a blue streak in the loaf, and the loaf itself used to run off the griddle, in spite of the best efforts of the careful intelligent women. And the potatoes were wet, tasteless, and without nourishment.

There were streets in Cork of the Harbours which were so full of the plague and disease that walls had to be erected at each end so that the healthy people couldn't go through them, just as is done in Turkey during a plague. (It is the Christians who do this in Turkey). But a thousand million thanks to the Great Almighty, no harm has been done to the crops in Ireland this year although the harvesting is slow.

September 11th . . . Last Thursday in Dublin Castle I heard a band playing music which was like the music of devils. The bassoons were like a sow crooning to her young. The musical pipe sounded like the squeeling of piglets. The flute sounded like a muffled fart, the trumpets and horns sounded like the laughter of fiends and the serpent like the sighing of demons, the trombone like the harsh cry of the heron. It wasn't soft like the love-notes of the heron. The clarinets were like the cry of the plover and the corncrake. It in no way resembled the sweet gently moving music of the Irish.

The Feast Day of St. Michael of the Rent, so called because the rent is collected today in most of Ireland. A fine thin-clouded sunny day. This is the Michaelmas Little Summer.

October 5th . . . A terrible war is on between the King of the Netherlands and some of his people who are Catholics . . .

The people now have leaders, and a treasurer collecting money to keep up the war against the King, William of Orange. The people of Hanover, Brunswick and Saxony are demanding their rights, that is freedom. There are many men raising their voices all over Europe with Daniel O'Connell. May God grant him success . . .

19th . . . A mild night, which I spent happily at Mícheál Ó hIcí's, eating luscious beef and fragrant mutton, and drinking sweet strong punch, until midnight, in the company of the parish priest and Risteard Codlatán, and the man of the house and his wife, who is the priest's sister.

23rd . . . The Catholic bishop, Dr. Kinsella visited us yesterday to solve the disagreement between the parish priest Fr. Séamas Hennebry and Fr. Seán Ó Deabhrán, who had made certain accusations against Fr. Hennebry with the encouragement of Risteard Ó Meachair, a shopkeeper, but important people of the town and myself defeated Ó Deabhrán in the presence of the Bishop, who said that the people of the parish had affection and respect for the parish priest and that he deserved it from them. Our Lord Bishop is a gentle and gracious person.

We had another meeting about the Lancastrian or Poor School and the Bishop arranged an agreement between the Catholics and the Protestants with regard to it.

25th ... The spalpeens were fighting at the Cross this Monday morning. A bull was being baited by dogs and by the ugly street rabble. I had a fine breakfast with Labhrás Green ...

28th ... Myself and another man went round collecting money to bury a poor woman from County Carlow. There is no other way to get a decent wooden coffin for a poor stranger in this land of the Irish since the foreigners came here. May they not last long here! It was they who destroyed Ireland and the Irish.

November 1st ... A shilling a day for a spade-worker. I spent part of the night at the parish priest's house drinking and enjoying myself. He is very grateful to me for getting the better of his enemy in the presence of our lord bishop.

5th ... This is how the country people divide the different times of day and night: 1. *Breacadh an lae .i. solas 'fear le tor'* (daybreak). 2. *An chéad chamhaoir den lá* (the first blush of Aurora). 3. *Deargmhaidin .i. fáinne an lae* (Aurora, the rosy blushes before sunrise. 4. *Éirí gréine* (sunrise). 5. *Lá glan .i. lá geal.* (Full day of a cloudy morning). 6. *Am céalachan do bhriseadh, 'vulgo' aimsir bhricfeast* (breadfast time). 7. *Am chrúite na mba* (cowmilking time). 8. *Maidin .i. ó bhreacadh an lae go meán lae* (morning). 9. *Meán lae* (mid-day). 10. *Am proinne, 'vulgo' aimsir dhinnéar* (dinner time, about one o'clock). 11. *Tráthnóna* (about three o'clock in the evening). 12. *Deireadh lae* (evening). 13. *Luí gréine* (sunset). 14. *Crónú lae* (twilight after sunset). 15. *Solas fear le tor* (the extreme of day immediately approaching absolute night). 16. *Aimsir chodach* (supper time, about eight o'clock). 17. *Oíche* (night). 18. *Urthosach oíche* (first shades of night). 19. *Tosach oíche* (first start of night). 20. *I bhfad san oíche nó láimh le meán oíche* (far advanced in night or near midnight). 21. *Meán oíche* (midnight). 22. *Céad ghlao an choiligh* (first cockcrow). 23. *An dara glao den choileach* (second cockcrow). 24. *Deireadh oíche nó teacht an lae* (approaching day).

7th ... I and seven others spent a most enjoyable night eating, drinking, dancing and singing at the priest's house. A calm dry night.

8th ... I dressed my son Amhlaoibhín in a small body-coat, and also Séamaisín, the youngest of the family.

We took possession of the Poor School today. There was a sewing mistress in the upper part of it. She wouldn't let us in, so we had to knock down a brick wall, force the door and break the lock. Fanny Ní Fhaoláin, the sewing mistress is a bitter hostile peevish hunchback.

10th ... It is customary to spill blood on St. Martin's Eve, namely, the blood of a goose or gander, a pullet or chicken, a duck or drake, a fat pig or large beef, a big ewe or a bleating kid, a lamb or sheep, or a shaggy goat, or some other good animal. It is a good old custom which should be kept up everywhere there is no butcher's meat to be had, and every strong farmer and well-off person should kill a sheep, a cow or a pig and divide it among the cabin-dwellers and God's poor. The poor spalpeen has his back to the bush today, and perhaps hasn't broken his fast.

24th ... I read that there has been a dreadful storm west in Galway, which scattered the corn from the haggards like wisps of straw. It knocked one chimney which crashed down through three floors. It drove the tide into cellars in which three people were drowned. This storm didn't reach Callan until Saturday morning, between two cock-crows. It came quickly eastwards from Galway to us. There was a dreadful storm in Limerick as well.

28th . . . I had a meal at the priest's house. There were six well-to-do people with him. Five women came to tea. We spent the evening pleasantly eating, drinking, singing and enjoying ourselves until ten o'clock.

December 25th . . . *Easter Sunday and Christmas Day are the two best days for the stomach* . . . A sung mass at six o'clock before day-break. Snow at one o'clock and throughout the day. The rabble in the town are throwing snowballs . . .

29th . . . Although Desart Court is three Irish miles away I could count every tree there, and almost every branch, the air is so clear that you would think they were very close to you. The distant mountains are also very clearly to be seen because of the purity and brightness of the air. This is the way artists paint landscapes on canvas, they make the part of the country which is close to them clear so that every hill, house and tree is visible, but the distant part they make dark or dark blue, and almost invisible. The distant mountain looks dark except during snow, but every field, wall, tree and bush can be seen on the mountain that is near. Every landscape painter should learn from nature.

The ice is four inches thick on the lakes. There's not a young fellow in Callan who is not enjoying himself kicking football or skating or throwing snowballs.

Slieve na mBan mountain is glorious at sunset. The Galtees are glorious after that. A moonlit frosty night.

DIARY 1831

January 6th ... Thursday, Twelfth Day. A fine calm cloudy day. A great crowd in Callan today. Hundreds of people seeking exemption from tithes or a reduction in them from the Protestant Minister, Seoirse Stephenson, but there were peelers and soldiers there to keep the tithe collector firm in his demands.

This agitation is going on through the county of Kilkenny for the last fortnight, but it is little use going to law with the devil when the court is held in hell. The law is on the side of the Ministers and the Protestant Parliament will make no change until it has no other way out. A similar agitation is going on in England (for example in Norfolk). In sixteen counties in England hay and corn stacks are being burned by the workers, who are being hanged and tortured, and deported to Botany Bay because of this arson. It is dire poverty that is forcing the people of Ireland and England to rise up against the law of the country.

23rd ... Thin-clouded day, without a ray of sun. A cold lively wind from the north-east and the north at the end of the day. Twenty-four people, myself among them, at a party in the priest's house.

29th ... A dark calm morning. A heavy fall of flaky snow began at eight in the morning. It fell straight down, not slantwise. It is extremely heavy at nine o'clock. Everything is covered in white. The black coal in the market is hidden under a white hood. It continued snowing until three o'clock in the afternoon, when it started to rain heavily. A terrible downpour at eight o'clock. This is the worst day this year. *All weathers are like summer up to Christmas, and there is no real cold until St. Brigid's Day. A day of snow and rain is the day that kills the blackbird.* I think there will be very few blackbirds to be heard singing next summer as the winter has killed them all.

31st ... This night will kill the birds. A sharp piercing blustery wind from the north. The tavern signs are rattling noisily. You would think the severe winter was having a final blow at us. Those living in poor empty ruins of houses, and the half-clad people of Ireland are to be pitied.

February 1st ... Every mountain, peak, hill and plain are under a thick covering of drift snow. The mail coach was late, and no wonder, because more snow fell around Dublin than near Callan. I wouldn't be surprised if the Ulster coaches are held up — the Belfast, Derry, Enniskillen and Coleraine coaches.

Much snow in every dike, furrow, and glen. The bushes on the sheltered side of the ditches are like white feathers, but the tops of the trees and branches are free of snow as they are shaken by the piercing whistling north wind. A cold snowy night.

4th ... A beautiful bright airy sunny blue-skied morning. A sharp piercing wind coming over frosted mountains, icy hills, white plains and glens, frozen lakes and cold wildernesses. The low well-thatched cottage in which there is food and fuel is the cosiest place. No house is as comfortable as a sod-walled straw-thatched house with a tight door, small windows, a big fire and a plentiful supply of food. *A small house with comforts is better than a large house with little food.* An airy pleasant frosty day. The street is frozen hard ...

7th ... A good pig market. A fine soft cloudy day. A slight wind from the south-west. The snow has gone except in a few dikes. The mail was brought from Dublin to Carlow on men's shoulders, and on horseback from there to Kilkenny, and in the mail coach from there to

Cork. I sold two pigs for six pounds eight shillings and bought a pig for one pound eighteen shillings. Muddy streets.

10th ... Fat Shrove Thursday. A heavy-clouded quiet soft morning. Dirty streets. The mail coach from Dublin came last night and again this morning. The road is now clear of snow ...

I read that the snow was as heavy in England as it was in Ireland. Two men were lost in the snow in County Wicklow. Three children died in the same place. The men's bodies have been found, but not the children's. Two people were suffocated between Dublin and Dún Laoire.

11th ... I hear the wild lark praising God in the sky today. I hear no other bird except the house sparrow ... *Every second day is fine and pleasant from Brigid's Day to Patrick's Day. All weather is fine from Brigid's Day on, the trout and salmon swim up to St. Mullin's.*

15th ... I hung five joints of meat, six ox-tongues and a half pig's head today.

Today is the day for cock-baiting. It was a barbarous custom. The cock used to be tied to a pole or stone pillar with a strong hemp cord, and sticks were thrown at it. It was given to the person who killed it. Each throw cost a penny. This barbarous custom has recently fallen into disuse. I haven't seen it for thirty years. It was an English custom. *Gallus* is the Latin name for cock and for Frenchman. Because of this the English took out on the poor cock the great hatred which they had for the French.

There was another common custom, betting on pitch-and-toss games, but that custom fell into disuse as did cock-baiting.

A good old custom still survives, that of baking oven-cakes by the rich, and giving them to the family and to the neighbours.

March 17th ... Patrick's Day ... Every pool is still full, as the proverb says: *If the pools aren't full before March, March itself will fill them* ... But of course the rest of the month will be fine and dry, according to the proverb: *Every second day fine and beautiful from Brigid's Day to Patrick's Day — every day from that on and half my own day* (said Patrick).

April 1st ... *Aoine an Chéasta* (Friday of Torture, Good Friday). It is so called because of the torturing of Christ on the Cross. A fine airy blue-skied sunny morning.

There is an old custom in Ireland, that of making a fool of people on April the First. I don't know what the origin of this silly custom is ... It is most inappropriate that April Fool's Day and Good Friday should fall on the same day.

I hear that Irish is the mother tongue in Montserrat in the West Indies since the time of Cromwell who transported some Irish people to the Island of Montserrat.[20]

20. Mention is made in contemporary Irish poetry of transportation, e.g. 'Transplú, transport mo mheabhair ar Bhéarla', V, 129 in O'Rahilly, *Five 17th Cent. Pol. Poems* (B.Á.C. 1952). Cf. also id. II, 94; III, 223; IV, 430.

For further information with regard to the Irish of Montserrat see: Gwynn 'Cromwell's Policy of Transportation', *Studies, XIX, 607; XX, 291;* Blake, 'Transportation from Ireland to America, 1653-60', *Irish Historical Studies,* III, 267; Gwynn, 'Irish in the West Indies', *Anal. Hib. IV,* 203.

The following letter was published in *The Athenaeum* (15/7/1905):
'Mount Verdon House, Cork, June 27th, 1905

With regard to the question which gave rise to the correspondence on the above subject, namely, the existence in the West Indies of negroes whose language shows traces of an Irish element, I have received—through the kindness of Mr. C. Cremen, Cork Harbour Commissioners' Office—the following information, which, though not perhaps absolutely conclusive, yet is most interesting. Mr. Cremen writes: "There is an old saying among our Cork sailors of the old sailing-vessel days, 'In Montserrat, where the blacks speak Irish'. He goes on to speak of the great trade in old days between Cork and the West Indies, of his personal

Irish is spoken commonly there by both whites and blacks. My heart goes out to the poor Irish deportees. Be they black or white I love the Irish people.

4th . . . Went to Dublin on the day coach. Left Callan at nine in the morning and arrived in Dublin at half-past nine at night. There was snow on the high peaks of *Fir Tuathail* that is, County Wicklow. It is a mountainous

knowledge of many of the sailors, and of the fact that all those he knew are now dead. He continues:

"None, indeed, of those I knew intimately were ever in Montserrat save *one*, John Donovan, lately in charge of Parnell Bridge (Cork), who died about eighteen months ago. He was a native of Ring, near Clonakilty, and spoke Irish very fluently. He frequently told me that in the year 1852, when mate of the brig Kaloolah, he went ashore on the island of Montserrat which was then out of the usual track of shipping. He said he was much surprised to hear the negroes actually talking Irish among themselves, and that he joined in the conversation . . . One phrase he stated to have been used by one of these negroes was very interesting from your point of view. He said the blacks were much astonished when he spoke to them, and one of them asked him (I write the Gaelic phonetically)".

Mr. Cremen here gives five Irish sentences, but did not send me the translation; if I get it in time I shall forward it. However, the sailor told the negro he came from Cork, and the black answered, "She sin Corcaig na g'cuan", i.e., "That is Cork of the Harbours". Mr. Cremen continues:

"This last remark of the negro was peculiar. 'Cork of the Harbours' is an old description long obsolete, and to be met with only in old poems and writings of about the time of Cromwell, so that he must have (had) the idioms and expressions of the earlier half of the seventeenth century very purely".

Now, with regard to Mr. Cremen's statements, it ought to be quite easy to find out in Montserrat whether the negroes really do or did speak some sort of Irish. Then, if they do, the question arises, How did Irish get there? Mr. Cremens suggests through fugitives from Barbados. Montserrat and Nevis both had English settlers before Cromwell's time *(Ency.Brit.)*.

Of course it may have come in by the emigration of Irish labourers to the West Indian estates of Irish or English merchants. I have never heard, however, of such emigration.

W. F. Butler'

county. There are many mountains there *'ag bagairt a gcinn thar dhroim a chéile'*. (Raising their heads threateningly above one another).[21]

6th ... Spent the day buying goods and paying money for them.

8th ... A calm foggy morning in Dublin. I left it at half-past eight and got to Kilkenny at six in the evening, that is, it took nine and a half hours to get from Dublin to Kilkenny. A quiet southerly wind. Took it easy walking home from Kilkenny to Callan. Although there was a good deal of rain we avoided it.

The Wake.

24th ... Up at three o'clock in the morning, walking through the fields. There was a wake on the Fair Green, but I wasn't there, for the Bishop has now forbidden young people and unmarried people to attend wakes at night. It is a good thing he has done, because the only

21. A line from Merriman's *The Midnight Court*.

pastimes they had at wakes were playing games such as 'The Dun-coloured Little Churl', 'The Lying Judge', 'Sir Straw', 'The Queen in Greece', and the likes; telling Fenian tales and singing throughout the night.

And of course, even if they weren't married, they knew something about courting.

A pleasant airy warm sunny day. A gentle breeze from the south. A large number of stallions on show in the street.

May 14th ... I had two men carting and spreading manure. I am **not** manuring the land in small **patches**, but covering it all **over**. I have a donkey **carting it, a** man in charge of it, and a woman setting potatoes in young Riocard de Búrc's land between Cúirt Phiarais and Droichead na nGabhar. Land in which potatoes were set is lumpy. I was breaking up the lumps with a mallet until I was very tired.

28th ... I have a black swallow with short, feathery, crooked legs, long wings and a white throat. Fatted calves on the market today. The front quarter at fourpence a pound, the back quarter at five pence a pound. This is cheap.

June 2nd ... Corpus Christi. Fair Day in Kilkenny in Munster. Beautiful fresh sunny day with blue skies and fleecy clouds. A warm wind from the south, with a heat haze coming up from the ground.

'Corpus Christi of the Fine Benches'. In olden times it was customary to spread fresh rushes and irises, etc. on benches near the doors of country houses, on which the old people used to sit telling Fenian tales. The young people would sit there listening to them, while the women lovingly fondled their babies.

23rd ... St. John's Eve. Fasting ... A bonfire and 'John's straw' on every high place

24th . . . Oats are liable to disease up to St. John's Eve, but some of it is already in ear and too short in the stalk. It will grow taller after the rain.

26th . . . Hurling, cock-fights, strolling, etc. on the Fair Green . . .

27th . . . Séamas Ó Loinsigh's wife from Droichead na nGabhar died in childbirth at eleven o'clock last night. She died suddenly a half an hour after giving birth to the child. This was the result of a fright she got when crossing the King's River near her house, with a tankard of milk on her head, after milking the cows. Her daughter also had a tankard on her head, and she slipped on the plank which crosses the deep pool, which is the result of taking out the stones to build the mill wall. The mother is being waked today, while the baby is lively and well and is being suckled by a nurse.

July 1st . . . This day two years ago my wife died. Her death was a lasting sorrow for me and my dear family. May the merciful God have pity on her soul. Amen, O Lord.

10th . . . Peggy St. John delivered of a daughter today . . .

12th . . . Máire is Peggy's baby's name . . .

16th . . . Peggy St. John and daughter left me today.

21st . . . Peggy St. John and her young daughter left me today. I believe she will never come back

23rd . . . 'May you be safe and sound and may God destroy your enemy' — I heard this from an old woman.

August 9th . . . My school consists of John Going, William Loughlan, Samuel Walker, 3 Shellys, Grainger,

Michael Keating, my own children and Murphy.

12th ... I saw a new attachment today on a scythe cutting oats for Seoirse Gliondún. A cradle was attached to the scythe as illustrated below. This scythe saves the crop, both straw and corn, as it cuts low and leaves the crop straight down in layers.

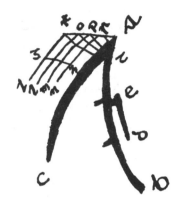

a, b: handle of scythe
d, e: grips
a, c: blade
a, f, i, n: cradle
fi, ol, pm, rn: slats of cradle, parallel to blade
ft, etc.: small iron rods to keep the back slat of the cradle tied firmly to the scythe.

A reaper using a cradle-scythe can cut as much oats or barley with it as four men would cut with a sickle. But the land must be free of mounds, depressions or ridges, and the corn even, not disturbed by storm. It would not be easy to cut wheat with this instrument, for it is usually tossed about because of the weakness of the stalks, the weight of the ears, and the length of time it takes to grow during stormy weather, and also because the narrow ridges are not made the same width on top in order that they might throw off the winter rain.

These two scythe-mowers are from Cill Train, otherwise Teampall Loisc. None of the scythe-men here are able to use this cradle-scythe nor have they got one. The cradle-scythe mowers are getting the pay of two men, namely, two shillings a day, and they are well worth it. *Cliabhspeal* (cradle-scythe) is the name of the implement, and *cliabhspealadóir* (cradle-scythe-man) the name of the man.

16th ... Thunder and lightning and a dreadful downpour after two in the morning. The downpour kept on for three hours, that is until five. The lightning was so bright that one poor person in Claí Mór thought his cabin was on fire. There are yellow torrents in every stream in Callan. The oldest inhabitant cannot remember such heavy rain. It went down to the yellow clay.

There was a cloud-burst or water spout in Gleann Fleisce, near Killarney, County Kerry, my native place. The floods swept away people, cattle, corn, turf and all the crops. The Killarney people stood terrified on the Fleisc Bridge watching the destruction, without any chance of assistance. Eight people from one house were swept away, the mother, father and six children. A great number of people were drowned. Their bodies are being found as the floods subside. Others were swept into Loch Léin, and they will never be found. This a sad story for the people of my poor native place.

A calm gentle cloudy morning. Eighteen pence and a glass of whiskey are the wages of a sickle reaper today.

20th ... Left Callan at three in the morning on my way to Clonmel. A soft dark morning. Mid-day and evening were sultry. The district between Clonmel and Gleann Bodhar is parched ...

I didn't get back to Callan till eleven. The moon was glorious in a blue sky without cloud or mist. Brought home a load of goods for Mí na nÓinseach.[22]

September 8th ... A fine calm thin-clouded sunny day. The Shelly's and the Keatings left my school. I broke up. I have no longer any school. Ceased teaching on the 8th Sept. when my school consisted of 3 Shellys, 2 Keatings, Townsend, Going, Walker and Grainger and Loughlan.

22. The author explains *Mí na nÓinseach* as follows: 'The month of the Vain Ladies', the month succeeding the cutting of the harvest when the Co. Kilkenny females buy clothes for the produce of their "Díoscán" money or Harvest money'.

19th . . . Seoirse Walker arrested **Pádraig Mac** Eochaidh by order of the court, at eleven o'clock last night. The street mob tried to recapture him, and they broke the window in Walker's door. He fired at them with a pistol. The peelers had to come out to save Walker's house from being broken up by the mob.

25th . . . Left Callan on the mail coach in an attempt to get to Dublin, but couldn't get further than Kilkenny, because of the number of well-to-do people who had been at the races, and had booked seats before me. I had to sleep in Kilkenny overnight. My bed cost me a shilling. A quiet moonlight night. A half-crown on the coach from Callan to Kilkenny.

26th . . . Left Kilkenny on the day coach. Six and sixpence is the fare from Kilkenny to Dublin. That is cheap. A fine thin-clouded calm sunny day. Arrived in Dublin at four in the afternoon, that is ten hours to cover fifty-seven miles. A fine calm night. I bought books.

28th . . . Michaelmas Eve. I bought goods and paid for them all in cash. A quiet rainy night.

29th . . . Michaelmas Day, Thursday. A fine soft cloudy day. Collected all my goods together at Duffy's warerooms in Lower Bridge Street and packed them in big bags tied with hard hempen ropes. A night of heavy rain. I had breakfast — beef and potatoes — for fourpence halfpenny. I ate some of the Michaelmas goose.

30th . . . Heavy clouds in the morning in Dublin, but they were lifting as we were getting away from the city, which we left at nine o'clock. A fine thin-clouded sunny day. A strong blustery wind from the south. *No storm as bad as one from a south wind*. We reached Kilkenny at six, that is, the journey took nine hours and a few minutes. I had a meal of bread and butter in Eibhlín Ní Dhulachanta's, my sister-in-law's house. I put a noggin of whiskey in a bottle and left Kilkenny at seven. There were a few drops of rain falling. It started to pour down on me at Garraí an Phíopa (The Pipe Garden), a field which was sold in the days of Cromwell for a pipefull of tobacco. It now grows tobacco. There are few fields now around Kilkenny where tobacco is not growing at present. It needs a lot of manure and a lot of care, and it is very profitable. But an act of the English Parliament has put an end to this crop. It is no longer possible to set any of it. It continued pouring rain on me from Garraí an Phíopa to Áth Choiléir, where I drank a drop from my little bottle. There was a strong southerly wind almost straight against me, but slightly from the left. Small showers were falling on me and the road was deep in mud. I kept on through Cnoc Gréine to Baile Mhac Dháith, where I drank another small sup and then on to Tulach Mhaoine where I had a tiny drop, then over Cnoc Riabhach to Caisleán Tóbain where I finished my little bottle of strong balsam. I was at the Market Corner in Callan at ten o'clock after suffering from much rain and the beating of the wind on my left cheek. Not a stitch of my clothes was dry.

October 4th . . . I went from Droichead na gCarbad, Magh Dheisil and the Islands to Magh Thobair. It was pouring rain when I was coming back. I called to Pádraig Ó Faoláin's at Crois, Teampall Mhagh Dheisil, where I had bread and butter and plenty of punch. As I passed near Droichead na gCarbad I had to go into a cabin where I was welcomed by a well-mannered gentle young woman, who sat up with me beside the fire until eleven o'clock when the downpour stopped, and I started to go home. The new road was flooded and I was up to my calves in water at every step. A severe dark night.

10th . . . Callan fair day. A fine soft quiet cloudy day. Many people, cattle, small pigs, birds, etc.; quantities of onions. Not a blow was struck, although there was great talk of fighting the day before the fair, but *there is often great darkness but little rain.*

Myself and my son Donncha were very busy selling goods in the shop.

26th ... The roof-laths and the slates of the Market House fell in after the troup of actors left. It was fortunate that they had left, for some of them would have been killed coming down the stone stairway, had there been a panic.

31st ... Spent the night pleasantly and quietly eating apples, burning nuts, drinking tea and punch and eating apple-pie. That is how I finished the Autumn season.

December 15th ... A fine soft cloudy day. Gentle wind from the west. A quiet cloudy moonlight night. A number of people were killed in the Walsh Mountains near Baile Hugúin yesterday. It is said that eighteen of the peelers accompanying Butler, who was serving citations to the Bishop's Court because of tithes due to Hamilton, the minister of Cnoc An Tóchair, were killed.

This is bad for the Irish, as the Protestants will wreak vengeance on them.

16th ... The funerals of three peelers came through Callan today.

17th ... A bitterly cold night. A fierce wintry howling stormy night. *No real storm is without a wind from the south.*

I pity the people of the Walsh Mountains to-night.

27th ... Two machine guns and their crew, and soldiers arrived today.

28th ... Went with carters to Clonmel today. A quiet

misty morning at three o'clock. The moon in the last quarter. Left Callan in a horse-cart at five o'clock. First signs of dawn came at Tigh na Naoi Míle; daybreak at Muileann na gCloch Chapel; the first blush of aurora at the opening of Glen Bodhar; rosy blushes before sunrise at the end of Glen Bodhar; sunrise shortly after that. The view of Gleann an Óir and the Commeraghs was beautiful.

'Peelers ... May their visit to us do them no good'. (p. 120)

The sky was clear of cloud or mist, smoke rising up out of the chimneys all around. A heavy mist fell when we were four miles from Clonmel. The meadows by the Suir were badly flooded and there was a thick fog over the river from Clonmel to Portlaw.

I bought a great amount of goods from Malcomson.

Left Clonmel at seven in the evening. Came through the fog for four miles on a muddy road, but after that the road was frozen hard for two miles. The next two miles the road was soft and muddy. The frost hardened at Glen Bodhar. It was very difficult to draw the carts. We were two hours doing one mile up this rough glen, and didn't reach Tigh na Naoi Míle until two in the morning. We stopped there and had a meal of bread and meat, and drank beer and whiskey. The frost was still hard as we went from Tigh na Naoi Míle towards Callan, but the road turned to mud at Poll an Chapaill. We reached Callan at seven o'clock.

DIARY 1832

January 11th ... Mid-day cold and wet with a west wind ... *Mind the cattle in spring after a fine winter.*

Sceithbholg is the crackling noise heard in harvest when the corn is ready to shell through exceptional heat and moisture and consequent ripeness.

23rd ... A fine soft cloudy day. Dirty streets. A good pig market. A mist and wind from the south in the morning and evening. Sunshine at mid-day. I never saw as many suckling piglets for sale as were in the market today.

A troup of actors are now performing in Callan.

25th ... My little bitch, Flora, killed a large rat which the cat had chased down from the third floor.

February 3rd ... Snow on every mountain and high hill. A sunny grey-blue sky till nine, but cloudy with a mist from that on.

Some people are ploughing stubble fields and digging them. Diggers are getting very small pay, four shillings for digging a quarter acre of stubble. Thirty-five shillings is the rent for a quarter acre of conacre stubble which was manured the year before last and in which wheat was sown last year.

4th ... The night as dark as Poll an Phúca in Ráth an Phúca (The Pooka's Hole in the Pooka's Rath).

A man called Burke was hanged last year in Edinburgh, the capital city of Scotland, for murdering thirty people by smothering them in order to sell their bodies to surgeons for ten guineas each. It has been discovered that thousands of people have been smothered in Edinburgh and London so that their bodies could be sold in this way. It is said that the same devilish practice now exists in Ireland. Rumour has it that there is a group of Burkers in Callan now, but I don't believe it. This is how they 'burke' a person: they pull a hood treated with pitch down over the mouth and nose, and thus smother the person. What they do in London and Edinburgh is to make the person drunk first, or put opium into his drink, and then smother him.

8th . . . The little thrush is singing sweetly on the branch in every sheltered bush; the wild lark happily singing high up in the sky, and many other birds enhance the beauty of the morning with their sweet song. The bright daisy, the yellow dandelion, the star-like celandine and the yellow flower of the furze adorn every glen. A fine soft quiet cloudy day.

9th . . . A bright sunny dewy blue-skied morning. The redbreast singing sweetly. The wagtail busy by the stream. There are two kinds of wagtail, the water wagtail and the grey wagtail. I see the waterhens near Inis na Giúise at O'Brien's Mill. The dandelion is resplendent. The catkins of the hazel are sprouting . . . a moonlight night.

Peggy St. John broke four window panes in my house today.

17th . . . Dáithín na nUbh (Little David of the Eggs, namely David Oldis) was buried today.

18th . . . Fishermen recognise the mayflies which are moving down the river now, for they are tying artificial mayflies to their hooks. They have a special artificial fly, each depending on the weather. A fine quiet warm night. One could sleep out of doors.

22nd . . . It is said that the tithes will be taken from the ministers who will be left only with their glebe-lands, for example Butler's glebe in Cill Dá Lua, near Callan, the Cill Bríde glebe, etc.

March 7th . . . *Céadaoin na Luaithre, is mór an*

buaireamh bainne d'ól (On Ash Wednesday there is a great temptation to drink milk). The judge and Daniel O'Connell are coming in to Kilkenny today. The Carraig Seac people will be on trial between this and Sunday. May Almighty God help them. Amen, O Lord! We shouldn't be without hope. A cold stormy night.

9th . . . I hear that the Carraig Seac prisoners have been released on bail, without trial and are to come before the autumn sessions.

10th . . . The Carraig Seac men were not let out on bail as was reported yesterday, but they are being kept in prison to be tried at the autumn sessions.

11th . . . The First Sunday of Lent, otherwise 'The Sunday of the Tears'. *A Shrove hen is no better than a May bush*. A great number of people walking up and down amusing themselves.

25th . . . The Feast of The Annunciation . . . O'Connell's rent collected in Callan today.

April 3rd . . . February oats (oats that are set in dry warm land at the end of February) are said to be best. Oats set in March and April are also good but 'cuckoo oats' namely oats set while the cuckoo is heard, are no good.

6th . . . Fifty artillery-men, together with trumpeters and horn-blowers came in to Callan today.

16th . . . *Meanadh* means foretelling, through itching in some part of the body. If on your right side, a man is coming to visit you; if on your left, a woman. An itching of the jaw means a stranger is coming to stay a while with you. Itching lips mean that you will get a kiss from a friend. An itching chin means that you will be drinking and enjoying yourself with friends. Itchy tears are a sign of sorrow and crying at a death. Itching in the shin or behind the knee portends walking. *I have the walking-itch — May your journey lead you to Limerick* (are well-known remarks). An itch in the breast means you will have a companion in bed.

Mist comes with every sort of weather. A mist for bad weather is on the mountains. Every corn field and level plain is now green. Milk will be plentiful. Instead of buying pints for a penny each from the pails, a quart is being bought from the churns. Veal will be cheap. Mutton is sixpence a pound, pork and beef are fivepence halfpenny. No lamb to be seen yet, but I see an odd kid. They will be plentiful on Easter Saturday.

26th ... The cholera morbus is killing hundreds in Dublin, Cork, London, etc., but it is in Paris that it is wreaking destruction. There, thirty thousand people have been struck down by it. They are being buried by night in the big ditch that surrounds Paris.

29th ... We had a meeting today to keep the cholera from Callan. May God help us.

May 4th ... Soldiers in Callan waiting for the collection of the tithes, although the new tithe law has not yet been enacted, that is the law enabling a process to be served on a person by putting his name up on the Protestant church door. The presence of these soldiers is like *Cró roimh na hairc* — building a sty before you have piglets.

5th ... Fourteen people in Graignamanagh, beside the Barrow at the foot of Cnoc Bréanaill in County Kilkenny, got cholera this week. Twelve of them died on the one day. This is great slaughter. This deadly plague is in Dublin, Cork, Naas, and in Tamhlacht Mhuintir

Pharthalóin. There has been four thousand years between the two plagues.[23]

7th ... I had four men digging potatoes at ninepence a day each, with food and drink. They did a good day's work.

8th ... Two women setting potatoes for me at sixpence a day each, with food and drink. Two women set a quarter of an acre a day.

9th ... Three men and a horse and cart were spreading manure for me today. The horse, cart and man in charge of it cost four shillings for the day. The land is as dry as a knot in timber.

June 11th ... The poor people of Ireland are very credulous. Some joker sent off a silly person with a burnt twig which had been quenched by water blessed at Easter and told him to divide it into four parts and to leave each part in a house, telling a person in each house that unless they did the same thing they would die from the cholera. In this way, sixteen people, then sixty-four, and then two hundred and fifty-six, 1,024, 4,096, etc. got this 'fire' with the result that they were a laughing-stock for the Protestants. The foolish men and women did a wonderful amount of running. Their faces were like a full moon and as red as blood from running. They used to tell in every village that the majority of the people in the village they had left were dead from the cholera. In Callan, it was said that the people of Gort na hUamha were dead, in Ceanannas it was the Callan people who had died. They didn't stop till they reached the sea. The foolish tale went

23. This is a reference to the *tamh* or plague from which Muintir Pharthalóin suffered in the year 2186, according to Keating's History, a manuscript copy of which Amhlaoibh possessed. He connects the word *támh* (=plague) with *Tamhlacht* (=a burial place), anglicised Tallaght.

through New Ross, Waterford, Kilkenny, Carrick-on-Suir and Clonmel. A woman asked me what she should do with the stick she had got. I told her to go and give it to the priest. 'Och', she said, 'he would whip me for it', and she went off home sadly, for she couldn't find four houses where she could leave her devilish magical black-burnt twigs. In some places it was a wisp of straw which had been burnt to a black magical dust and dipped in wireworm water, that is water which people think kills wireworms. These are worms which eat corn in the blade. Although this is a barbarous business, it goes to show that it takes little encitement to move the Irish to good or to evil.

Some people say it was the ministers who were responsible for starting this in order to have revenge for the non-collection of tithes because of the concerted action of the Irish against them.

18th . . . The cholera morbus is wreaking destruction in Ennis, Limerick and Tullamore. I am told it is in Passage near Waterford. There is a Health Board in Callan consisting of thirteen members, one of whom I am. We must clear the town of dung heaps, etc.

19th . . . The charm against evil: *Three who do harm, man, woman and an evil fairy. Three who guard against them, the Father, the Son and the Holy Spirit.*

20th . . . Sixty peelers came to Callan today on their way to collect tithes in Co. Wicklow. They came from the counties Tipperary, Cork and Kerry. May their visit to us do them no good!

26th . . . I am in charge of seven men and two horses and carts carting stones and yellow clay to fill holes in Mill Lane to prevent cesspools bringing the cholera to Callan. We are taking the yellow clay and the stones from the Market Corner, near the barracks. This corner badly needed widening, because the mail coach often turned over there.

28th ... Seán Ó hAithiarainn, the son of the baker, is now in charge of the men and the horses at the Market Corner. Séamas Mac an Eidhre brought us a cold drink of oatmeal and water. Straw for bedding is being given free to Callan's paupers, and the old straw and the fleas are being thrown out. Every dung heap and cesspool is being cleared. Fear of the cholera has done us that much good.

Many John's fires alight over the county to-night. It is very pleasant watching them from the Fair Green and listening to the cries of the groups around them. The voice of the corncrake is pleasant, for no other bird calls alone in Ireland, except the grey plover in winter.

July 8th ... A fine day. Bright and short hot periods. I was at a meeting in Baile Héil, near Cloch an Tóchair and Carraig Seac. There were at least a hundred thousand men present. There were twenty thousand horsemen at it. Men came from Wexford and Tipperary to oppose the tithes and church rates and demanding the return of the Parliament to Dublin. I spoke there in Irish.

10th ... St. John's Fair day. A fine day, with bright periods and short hot spells. Many people, animals and goods at the fair. No quarrelling or fighting except among a few brats at the end of the day. I and my family, Donncha, Anastás, Amhlaoibh and Seamas sold an amount of goods. A fine fresh night. A full moon.

24th ... The Carraig Seac men have been freed. The judge released them today. He couldn't find a jury in County Kilkenny which would find them guilty. There are thousands of bonfires on the hills of Ireland all around as far as I can see on Sliabh na mBan, hundreds of fires on Sliabh Díle, on the Walsh Mountains, on Sliabh Ardach, on the Crannach Hills, on every hill and mountain in the four counties, Kilkenny, Tipperary, Waterford, Wexford, and of course on Carraig Seac itself.

August 23rd . . . Left Callan between one and two in the morning after the western-horned moon had risen. A sharp west wind, the aurora borealis bright in the north. Went through Áth an Iúir, Áth an tSearraigh, Coill na bhFraochán, Garraí Uí Rícin, Gleann Bodhar Gap, etc. to Clonmel, which I reached at seven in the morning. I bought two hundred pounds worth of goods.

As a result of the cholera the country people are no longer buying or selling in Clonmel. I left Clonmel at ten at night. Musicians were playing on the streets to keep up the spirits of the people. The aurora borealis gave me light during the night. Day broke when I was at Cill Lamhraí. I came home and went to sleep after staying up for two nights.

31st . . . A salmon for breakfast. I am taking in seven pounds a day in the shop this week, as the people of Gabhal Mhaí and of Crannach, etc. who used to go shopping to Kilkenny are now coming to Callan.

May Callan keep clear of cholera for a long time.

September 1st . . . Kilkenny is in a very bad state with the cholera. William Mac Cormaic, the solicitor, died suddenly of it yesterday. He was buried this morning in Leaca na Cuaillí Móire, his family burial ground. A doctor buried him, as nobody else would do it for fear of the cholera. One hundred and fifteen people have caught the fever in Kilkenny. Only eleven of them have recovered, seventy of them died, and the rest are still ill . . .

2nd . . . A fine soft thin-clouded morning with no sunshine. Every day is the same. This is truly the Michaelmas Little Summer . . .

28th ... Nurse Moore gave up the child to Peggy St. John.

November 25th ... Beginning and middle of month fine. Seed being sown. The end of the month wet and wintry. The cholera came to Callan at the beginning of the month. Twenty people went down with it, and it left the town then.

26th ... A fight between the Soldiers (74th battalion) and the country boys.

27th ... Pádraig Ó Deabhrán sent to prison today for his part in the fight with the soldiers yesterday.

Faction Fighting.

January 2nd . . . Pól Céitinn died this morning and was buried in the evening. It is thought that he died of the cholera. The town rabble were mad drunk at his funeral.

21st . . . Two died of the cholera at Sceach an Chloithreán, that is, Brian na gCis ('Brian of the Baskets') and his wife.

23rd . . . Two were buried today, Cáit Ní Chonaill and Murchadha the Feather Dealer. They both had drunk as much as a giant would in the cholera hospital yesterday, and they died last night. It's a short time either of them got for repentance. North-east wind.

31st . . . No deadly cholera in Callan today. Three young girls are going about with the *brídeog* (effigy of St. Brigid).

February 27th . . . Coercion bill against Ireland in the Parliament.

March 2nd . . . A peeler took a shot at a person in Callan today, but he hit a horse which died shortly afterwards.

3rd . . . Major Brown, the inspector of the peelers came today to examine people who had complained about the peeler who killed the horse yesterday. The major paid the owner, Britt from Dair Mhór, ten pounds, and sent the peeler to Kilkenny prison to stand his trial before the justice on the ninth of this month.

Commenced at T. Corr's, teaching at 10 shillings per month.

25th . . . Eighteen members of the 'Whitefeet' passed through today under a guard of soldiers on their way to Botany Bay.

April 8th . . . A rough fight between the Townsends and others in the street. They were throwing stones at each other.

12th . . . The first of the days of the old brindled cow. A fine dry bright sunny day. A sharp north wind. Martial law is now in force in Kilkenny.

15th . . . Nobody has been arrested in Callan under martial law which was brought into force on the 11th of this month and I hope nobody will.

20th . . . The martial law was brought in with the express purpose of getting the tithes collected.

July 10th . . . St. John's Fair Day, that is, the fair held on St. John's Day, according to the old reckoning. Quiet drizzly morning. Fine cloudy day. The rowdies were fighting. The peelers shot a woman gingerbread seller in the hip and they injured one or two others.

11th . . . A fine quiet cloudy day. A large number of drunks about the streets.

August 17th . . . Ceased teaching at Mr. James Corr's. Mr. James Corr to H. O'Sullivan:
To tuition commencing March 4th 1833 and ending Augt. 17th 1833: £2.15.0.

23rd . . . Pay for sickle-reaper varied greatly this morning, thirteen pence, sixteen pence, four fourpenny bits, three sixpenny bits, five fourpenny bits, according as the wind got stronger and shook the crops. The late man wasn't at a loss . . .[24]

September 9th . . . Went for a swim at one o'clock. The

24. A play on the proverb *Bíonn an fear deireanach díobhálach*, the late man loses out.

water was warm. End of the day cloudy and cold. I hope to God we will soon get rain. Drizzly night.

29th . . . Went to Kilkenny and returned home at nine. I was looking at the cathedral and the new Butt's chapel. The latter is very beautiful inside and outside.

October 17th . . . Much wheat being sown by spade and shovel. Salmon twopence a pound.

28th . . . Seán na Gealaí Ó Donnchú was drowned last night in a ditch in Gráig Amhlaoibh, on his way home to Doirín, which is beside Desert Court. It appears that he was drunk, which was not unusual for him. He got the name Seán na Gealaí (Seán of the Moon) because he had a habit of not leaving Callan of the Ructions to go home on dark nights until the moon rose. He used to say 'I'll go home by moonlight'. Alas, he was drowned last night when the moon was full and he had plenty of moonlight. There was no light in his eyes, as he had drunk too much whiskey and beer. He was a son of Éamann Gearr Ó Donnchú from Doirín. He was called Seán na Gealaí in his youth, for it was thought he was a 'geilt' (lunatic), that is, a person under the influence of the *gealach* (moon).

29th . . . Seán na Geallaí was buried today in Cill Molua. The 'summer fallows' have been sown, but the land in which there has been a second crop of potatoes will be sown later. There are three sorts of fallow land.

Branar samhraidh, poor land which is ploughed, not sown, but left to be turned twice in summer, and is later sown at Michaelmas. This usually yields a good crop.

Branar soipín, wheat stubble ploughed, in which wheat is sown soon after it is cropped. This rarely yields a good crop.

Branar dubh, very poor summer fallow, which is left without seed during the winter and in which oats are sown in the following spring. This usually yields a good crop of oats.

November 4th ... Small pigs and piglets sold at poor prices. I saw a piglet go for two shillings. The people are frightened into getting rid of them for fear they would eat the potatoes on them. Some people digging potatoes. Four fourpences for men and a shilling for women per day digging them. That is good pay, if it lasts a good while.

6th ... Fourteen pence and a glass of whiskey for spadesmen digging potatoes ...

17th ... Paid M. St. John up to Nov. 1833.
O'Connell Sunday. Misty morning. Fine cloudy day. Thirty pounds was collected in Callan parish today. *Every weather like summer till Christmas.*

25th ... St. Catherine's or Caitilín's Feast. Fine bright blue-skied sunny day.
Some people say that Duibhré na Samhna (the November Dark Period) begins with the November full moon. Others hold that the 'Dark Period' is during the last quarter of the moon and it is with the latter that I agree. How could the full moon be called a 'dark period'? The moonless period comes only for about three days at the end and three days at the beginning of each month, that is, for one week. The first new moon that comes after St. Caitilín's Day or on St. Caitilín's Day, is called *Ré na Féil Caitilín* (the Moon of the Feast Day of Caitilín). A beautiful fresh quiet frosty night. Full moon.

26th ... I hear a strange story about the heron, namely that it is fattest when the moon is full, and thinest during the new moon, and that it grows fat as the moon waxes and grows thin as it wanes. This stands to reason in populous countries like Ireland, for the heron can fish every moonlit night, and sleep during the day, but during the moonless period it must fast almost every day for fear of its many human enemies who are hunting it, and it cannot fish during the darkness of night. Therefore it is thin during the moonless period and fat during the moonlight period. The same applies to all birds who live on night work, e.g. the snipe, the grey plover, the green plover and the woodcock, which are easier to shoot during the moonless period than during the moonlit period.

December 6th ... I read that many ships were sunk on the Irish and British coasts, on last Thursday and Friday, the 28th and the 29th — the same time as the slates were blown off my roof. A large number of sailors and merchants were drowned. The proverb *Every weather like Summer till Christmas* has been disproved and of course last week was wintry enough.

14th ... Paid M. St. John up to 14th Dec.

20th ... *Féil* means 'vigil'. In olden days among the Christians the 'day' began at sunset and lasted through the night till next sunset and they used to keep a vigil of the Blessed Sacrament from sunset on Easter Saturday till sunrise on Easter Sunday. Later on it became the custom to keep the same vigil from sunset before every feast day. This is why *Oíche Nollag* (Christmas Night) is the name of the night before Christmas Day, etc., for the night before the feast day was part of the natural day or day-and-night. Later still the custom was to keep this vigil all during the day before the feast, so that the whole day-and-night before Christmas was called *Oíche Nollag* (Christmas Night). The same applies to November Night. St. John's Night (that is, the night of the bonfire), St. Martin's Night, and so on with every day-and-night before a feast day or fixed day such as May Night. But when speaking of any other day, that is, Sunday night, the 'night' is understood to refer to the night following the named day.

24th . . . Fine weather badly needed, as most of the poor country cabins, especially those beside hills or mountains, have both the wet dripping from the roof and the wet oozing up from the floor.

January 3rd . . . God called the light 'day' and the darkness 'night', and the evening and morning were the first day. God made two large lights, the larger light, the sun, to rule the day, and the lesser one, the moon, to rule the night. From this it is to be understood that the 'day' is from sunrise to sunset, and the 'night' is from sunset to sunrise. We have light from the moon before sunrise and after sunset, and this light is called twilight, but day-and-night is called 'day'.

6th . . . 'Monday of the Good Women', or Twelfth Day, a holiday . . . Everything is damp and soggy now. Bacon is going soft in the chimney, and hung beef is the same. Dripping through the roof and oozing wet floors in every cabin. End of a day of rain. The south wind changed and a storm rose with a west wind and cold rain at the beginning of the night. The night is dark as the Pooka's Hole. The town rabble fighting each other.

10th . . . Fr. Séamas Hennebry who died of apoplexy, a sudden attack which leaves a person unconscious and sometimes kills him, was buried today. On Wednesday morning, after he had got up and was about to dress, he lost consciousness and collapsed on the floor. Nobody heard him fall, and he was dead before Dr. Céitinn arrived.

Young and old, big and small are weeping after him. The small children are crying over his tomb in the chapel, for he was a kind childlike priest among them. He was generous at his own table and he was lively spirited company, easily satisfied with regard to money, although it is said that he had plenty of it.

May the Great Almighty God have mercy on his soul, and may He take him forever to Heaven.

11th . . . Fine dry weather is badly needed, as the country

is flooded and the yellow clay is gushing up through the dirty streets of 'Callan of the Ructions'. If it ever was 'Callan of the Ructions', it certainly is now, for cursed crowds on either side of the King's River are throwing stones at each other, every Sunday and holiday night — the Caravats on the south side, especially around the Fair Green, Sráid na Faiche, Sráid an Mhuilinn and Sráid an Ghoráin, and the Shanavests on Faiche na nGard, Shepherd's Street or Lána na Leac and on the Kilkenny Road. If they are not stopped, someone will be killed . . .

14th . . . The first warm day this winter . . . I think the weather is improving and settling.

25th . . . Paid M. St. J. up to Jan. 25 . . .
The deadly illness, the cholera morbus, is in Callan again. Four have died already of it, and two are in the throes of death.

26th . . . Seven died of the deadly disease in the last three days. Two others are very ill with it . . .

February 1st . . . Fr. Séamas Hennebry left a lot of money to the poor of Callan. His was a hedgehog's store. *The grave's mouth often fed the poor's mouth.* A large number of mattresses came from Kilkenny together with forty pounds to support a hospital which was established today in the school house at Loch Buí.

9th . . . The disease is deadly . . . Forty-four have died of the deadly disease within the last eighteen days. Seventy-six fell ill. The well-off people are helping us in the time of our need.

March 12th . . . I spent the day hunting hares with two hounds, one white and the other spotted. We raised eight hares, although we killed only two. We walked ten miles towards Ceapach Éidín, Droichead na gCarbad and Baile na síg, Mícheál Óg Ó hAithiarainn, Uilliam Óg Báicéar and Seán Óg ÓTiarna from Baile Mág were in the party. Hunting is a fine lively pastime.

20th . . . I bought thirteen shillings worth of manure, which I spread on the Fair Green.

26th . . . A great number of people in Callan about the tithes. It almost came to a fight between the people and the peelers.

27th . . . Spent the night very foolishly in the company of Tomás Tóibín from Coill na bhFraochán and with M. St. J. May it do me no good!

May 1st . . . Fine blue-skied sunny May day. Bright and calm. The day coach horses are covered with beautiful flowers. The car-horses are the same. People working hard.

8th . . . Ascension Thursday. A holiday. Pádraig Ó Ceallacháin's funeral was held today. He died as a result of falling out of his cart on his way home from Kilkenny. The Ballingarry Shanavests came and the Callan Caravats attacked them. But the Shanavests put the Caravats to flight in their own town. Two were badly injured, a Shanavest and a Caravat. This is bad behaviour on a solemn feast day.

9th . . . Caisín, the Shanavest from Grágach is ill and weak and the Caravat from the Fair Green is ill and bruised.

14th . . . I set a quarter acre of cup potatoes in Rector Stephenson's land at Cúirt an Fhaoitigh.
   I spent the beginning of the night with Tomás Tóibín and [   ].

29th . . . Corpus Christi. A holiday. Kilkenny fair day. A fine fresh sunny warm day. Bright blue skies. Pigs were dying with the heat at the fair yesterday.

June 3rd . . . I am setting potatoes in manure and covering them with earth from the furrows. This is good weather for the potatoes, but I see wireworms eating the barley which was sown a month ago. I am greatly afraid that they will destroy my potatoes. I see birds (e.g. crows, robins, etc.) taking the wireworms in their beaks to their young. But for the birds of the air, the insects of the earth would eat every crop. Therefore the small birds do a lot of good, and of course, even if they eat a little of the corn, they are worth their work.

23rd . . . St. John's Eve . . . I saw no good bonfires, because the Coercion Bill forbids them.

24th . . . St. John's Day, the feast day of John the Baptist. This used to be always a holy day until today, but now the Church has ended that, because it used to be a great day for drinking after the bonfire night.

July 7th . . . We began to repair the streets in Callan and kept at the work for five weeks. We repaired from one end of the town to the other, that is, from Fíochán's Forge on the north side to the Milestone at the Chapel on the south. It was a great relief to the poor. I was in charge of them all the time. Every man and boy got ninepence a day. The end of the day showery.

August . . . On the 20th, Wednesday, a crowd of men and women went to cut barley without pay for Dean Stephenson. After coming home there was a fight between two sections of them, and between other Caravats and Shanavests. The peelers fired on them and Mac Éilí from Faiche na nGard was shot and killed. Mícheál Priut from Ballingarry was wounded and he died after a week. It was a good thing that a lot of the Shanavests were not killed at the funeral. They would have been but Major Brown did not allow the peelers fire on them.

Eight men have been sent to Kilkenny gaol — Labhrás Priut (a tenant's son), Fuíteach (a spalpeen), two Coinneacháns and Slatra (three fairly well-off persons), Éamann Éadmhard (shoemaker). Those six are Shanavests. Teddy Desinn, a Protestant weaver, Neddy Vass, a spalpeen. These two are Caravats.

December 23rd . . . A large quantity of meat at low prices but little was bought. The best pork and beef at threepence a pound; mutton at fourpence . . .

The people who took land during the Napoleonic War are surprised that the crops are now cheap, but they will have to do with low prices from this on.

27th . . . Máire Ní Airní, Séamas Ó hAirní's widow, was arrested for debt, and sent to Kilkenny Marshalsea (prison).

DIARY 1835

January 1st ... Little Christmas Day ... *God's right hand this year towards us!* May God grant us a happy year.

4th ... Fine soft cloudy day. Not a puff of wind. No cold, not a drop of rain. A fine soft mild night. Nobody ever saw finer weather at this time of the year.

31st ... No living person ever saw such a fine winter as this.

February 2nd ... Pig market ...

> There are brown prolific pigs,
> Black handsome pigs,
> Spotted pigs that fill the sty,
> Grey unwanted pigs,
> And thin dun-coloured pigs like goats,
> But a sturdy wide-backed light-headed pig
> Is the pig for me.

March 10th ... The whole country is covered with snow which fell last night with a west wind. Thin clouds in the morning. The sun shining weakly.

The catkins have come on the white willow and on the alder. A fine soft day of snow. The day ended with rain and a lively wind from the south west. Night began with a downpour. This is *corrach na bliana,* the time of the year when the weather is changeable.

25th ... Ellen Tracey came as a maid to me today at four shillings a quarter.

April 1st ... April Fools' Day. A barbarous custom from the time of the pagans is still observed in Ireland, that is, the custom of making an April Fool of a person. In the time when Venus was adored, the first day of the month was a feast in her honour, and it was usual to honour her by all sorts of lowly antics. But I think it is time to give up this pagan practice.

14th . . . There was a fire on the top of Suí Finn mountain last night. The fire near Carraig Seac was a mile long. I think that it was a furze-covered hill which was set on fire to celebrate the fact that Peel was defeated and that the tithes were abolished. On Sunday night there were thousands of fires, one on every height, hill and mountain as numerous as the stars in the heavens on a frosty night.

It will be fine if a war doesn't start between the Irish and the foreign ministers and their followers. A fine soft day. Dust on the roads.

A stretch of a hundred and fifty miles of hills and mountains all around the Glen was aflame, as far as I could see from Cnocán an Éithigh at the end of the Fair Green in Callan of the Ructions.

18th . . . At the market I see brushes made of heather and brushes made of the shrub on which the whortle-berry grows. It is called *duilliúr* from the broad leaf *(duilliúr)* that grows on it. The leaf that grows on the heather is very narrow, and no berry grows on it, but a small purple flower does. Both are shrubs, but are dissimilar. *Fraoch* (heather) is the *erica vulgaris,* and *duilliúr* is *vaccinium myrtillus.*

24th . . . I see barley being sown with an iron rake. Two men are drawing the rake and a number of young boys and girls are setting the seed.

May 3rd . . . Hurling match on the Fair Green. The youth of Callan strolling around the Green.

15th . . . I hear the cuckoo for the first time — and in my right ear. Silly people say that this brings luck, but that is only nonsensical talk.

28th ... Hurling, cockfighting and the long dance or 'High Gates', and cricket on the Fair Green. There are two kinds of hurling, namely, Irish hurling which is played with a stick and ball which is driven through the field, and through the goal or loop at the end of the field; cricket, that is, English hurling played with a bat and a ball which is thrown by hand to knock down a little gate, if possible, but the man with the bat defends the gate.

June 22nd ... I went to Cill Mhinic to Stacach's funeral. He was buried today in Stún Chárthaigh. Cill Mhinic is a very nice place in the summer. It is a small village on the commonage, with willows growing in profusion around every house.

23rd ... I went with Grace, a printer from Dublin to the Earl's woods at Desart Court, three miles from Callan. We went into the woods at Clais an Dair Mhóir. These woods are very pleasant. We walked on, telling stories about the little people, little foolish fairies, six inches in height, like the people of Lilipiusia. They wear red trews and caps, and short green jackets. They have a green circle in the Cnoc na Carraige woods at Baile Uí Chaoimh, and they dance there to fairy music every moonlight summer's night until the cock crows, when they vanish like a mist. Each leprechaun carries a purse full of gold hanging from his hand and on a hot day when a scythe-man sees them running through the meadow he tries to catch one to get the purse from him. The leprechaun is a ventriloquist and the scythe-man hears a wild rough voice behind him and when he turns around to see where the voice is coming from the leprechaun is swallowed down through the ground into the Land of Youth.

We walked through Doirín, and the Circle of Trees to Raven's Oak, and along the fish ponds to Desart Court, the big house, and then for a mile through the shrubbery, through the four-acre field which is enclosed by a seven-cornered wall, and through the glasshouse, on to Baile Uí Gheibhle, where I left my companion, Grace, the printer from Dublin. I came home by Tulach Mhaoine hill, and Cnoc Riabhach to Callan of the Ructions, having walked five miles by road, and another five through fragrant woods, beautiful shrubberies and green level fields. All that is needed to make Desart Court as fine a place as any in the world is a large river or lake ...

24th ... Yesterday in Doirín I saw house-walls made entirely of sally rods. It is from houses like these that Armagh is called Droim Saileach (The Sally Ridge).

July 12th ... I see Pádraig Ó Deabhrán from the Fair Green, who was fighting on fair day and was arrested by peelers, on his way now to prison in Kilkenny, with no hat on his head, or breeches on his fork, or stocking or boot on his feet. He well deserves it ...

21st ... I went to Dublin to buy goods. Spent a day going and six days in Dublin and a day coming home, that is, I was away from home for eight days. I went by the Carlow road and came back by the Athy road. It was very warm in Dublin, and on the journeys.

21st ... The coaches travel seven Irish miles an hour on the Athy road, and six on the Carlow road.

29th ... A pleasant fresh warm day. Went swimming.

30th ... A fine bright warm day. Sun and blue skies.

31st ... The same.

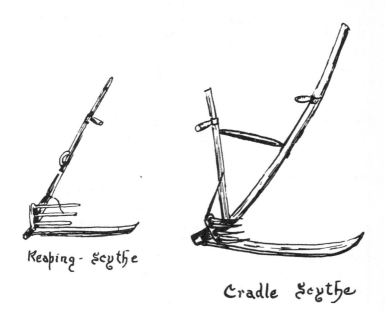

Reaping - Scythe

Cradle Scythe

Samples of scythes (see page 108) from *Old Farm Implements*, Wright, published by Adam & Charles Black.

More Mercier Bestsellers

MY VILLAGE – MY WORLD

John M. Feehan

This is a book that never palls or drags. It is boisterous and ribald and I am tempted to say that it is by far the funniest book I have ever read. It is also an accurate and revealing history of rural Ireland half a century ago and more. John M. Feehan writes beautifully throughout. I love this book.

From the Foreword by John B. Keane

My Village – My World is a fascinating account of ordinary people in the countryside. It depicts a way of life that took thousands of years to evolve and mature and was destroyed in a single generation. As John M. Feehan says 'Nobody famous ever came from our village. None of its inhabitants ever achieved great public acclaim ... The people of our village could be described in government statistics as unskilled. That would be a false description. They were all highly skilled, whether in constructing privies or making coffins, digging drains or cutting hedges, droving cattle or tending to stallions ... I do not want to paint a picture of an idyllic village like Goldsmith's phony one. We had our sinners as well as our saints ...'

The Man from Cape Clear
A Translation by Riobárd P. Breatnach of
Conchúr Ó Síocháin's *Seanchas Chléire*

Conchúr Ó Síocháin lived all his days on Cape Clear island, the southern outpost of an old and deep-rooted civilisation. He lived as a farmer and a fisherman and his story vividly portrays life on that island which has Fastnet Rock as its nearest neighbour. He was a gifted storyteller, a craftsman and a discerning folklorist. Here he tells of life on the island drawing on the ancient traditions and the tales handed down from the dim past. There is a sense of humour, precision and a great sense of community on every page.

The Man from Cape Clear is a collection of memories and musings, topography and tales, and contains a fund of sea-faring yarns not to be found elsewhere. It discloses aspects of insular life which should delight the inner eye of the world at large and enrich every Irishman's grasp of his heritage.

Ó Síocháin died in February 1941 and is buried beside Teampall Chiaráin on the island.

THE TAILOR AND ANSTY
Eric Cross

"Tis a funny state of affairs when you think of it'. It is the tailor himself speaking. 'This book is nothing but the fun and the talk and the laughter which has gone on for years around this fireside ...'

The Tailor and Ansty was banned soon after its first publication in 1942 and was the subject of such bitter controversy that it may well have influenced the later relaxation of the censorship law. Certainly it has become a modern Irish classic, promising to make immortals of the Tailor and his irrepressible foil, his wife, Ansty, and securing a niche in Irish letters for their Boswell, Eric Cross.

The Tailor never travelled further than Scotland and yet the width of the world can hardly contain his wealth of humour and fantasy. Marriages, inquests, matchmaking, wakes – everything is here. Let the Tailor round it off with a verse of a ballad:

Now all you young maidens,
Don't listen to me
For I will incite you to immortalitee,
Or unnatural vice or in a similar way
Corrupt or deprave you or lead you astray.

THE RED-HAIRED WOMAN
and Other Stories

Sigerson Clifford

'He blamed Red Ellie for his failure to sell. She stood before him on the road that morning, shook her splendid mane of foxy hair at him, and laughed. He should have returned to his house straightaway and waited 'till she left the road. It was what the fishermen always did when they met her. It meant bad luck to meet a red-haired woman when you went fishing or selling. Everyone knew that ...'

'This collection of stories has humour, shrewd observation, sharp wit at times, and the calm sure touch of an accomplished storyteller ... '
From the Introduction by Brendan Kennelly.

Each of 'Sigerson Clifford's delicious tales ... in *The Red-Haired Woman and Other Stories* is a quick, often profound glimpse of Irish life, mostly in the countryside. The characters appear, fall into a bit of trouble and get wherever they're going without a lot of palaver. The simple plots glisten with semi-precious gems of language ...'
James F. Clarity, **The New York Times Book Review**

'Flavoured by the wit and sweetness of the Irish language, this slender volume presents brief affectionate glimpses of Irish country life.'
Leone McDermott, **Booklist**

LETTERS FROM THE GREAT BLASKET

Eibhlís Ní Shúilleabháin

This selection of *Letters from the Great Blasket,* for the most part written by Eibhlís Ní Shúilleabháin of the island to George Chambers in London, covers a period of over twenty years. Eibhlís married Seán Ó Criomhthain – a son of Tomás Ó Criomhthain, *An tOileanach (The Islandman).* On her marriage she lived in the same house as the Islandman and nursed him during the last years of his life which are described in the letters. Incidentally, the collection includes what must be a unique specimen of the Islandman's writing in English in the form of a letter expressing his goodwill towards Chambers.

Beginning in 1931 when the island was still a place where one might marry and raise a family (if only for certain exile in America) the letters end in 1951 with the author herself in exile on the mainland and 'the old folk of the island scattering to their graves'. By the time Eibhlís left the Blasket in July 1942 the island school had already closed and the three remaining pupils 'left to run wild with the rabbits'.

It must be remembered when reading these letters that they were written in a language foreign to Eibhlís whose native language was Irish. Only very minor changes were thought desirable in the letters and these in the interests of intelligibility. Here, through the struggling idiom and laboured passages, emerges in fascinating detail a strange and different way of life as seen unconsciously through the eyes of a woman. This is not the island of the summer visitor but one intimately known, loved and feared – and finally abandoned.